WALK IN THE WILDERNESS

Torn Curtain Publishing
Wellington, New Zealand
www.torncurtainpublishing.com

© Copyright 2022 Shaneen Bruss. All rights reserved.

ISBN Softcover 978-0-6453977-5-8
ISBN EPub 978-0-6453977-6-5

No portion of this book may be reproduced, stored in a retrieval system or transmitted in any form or by any means—electronic, mechanical, photocopy, recording or otherwise—except for brief quotations in printed reviews or promotion, without prior written permission from the author.

Unless otherwise noted, all Scripture quotations are from the New King James Version®. Copyright © 1982 by Thomas Nelson. Used by permission. All rights reserved.

Cataloguing in Publishing Data
Title: Walk in the Wilderness
Author: Shaneen Bruss
Subjects: Personal memoir, Christian living, Prayer, Spiritual growth, Cultural heritage, Family relationships

Typeset in Minion Pro and Aviano Serif.

A copy of this title is held at the National Library of Australia.

WALK IN THE WILDERNESS

SHANEEN BRUSS

For I know the thoughts that I think toward you, says the Lord, thoughts of peace and not of evil, to give you a future and a hope.

Jeremiah 29 v 11

CONTENTS

Introduction 1
Preface 5
Chapter One 7
Chapter Two 21
Chapter Three 37
Chapter Four 49
Chapter Five 63
Chapter Six 77
Chapter Seven 93
Chapter Eight 109
Chapter Nine 121
Chapter Ten 135
Author's Note 139
Meditations from God's Word 143
Acknowledgements 155

INTRODUCTION

This is the story of the first forty years of my life. That number feels significant to me. Jesus spent forty days in the wilderness, and in all that He faced and endured in that time, I see my journey... my own walk in the wilderness. When Jesus came out from the wilderness after those forty days, He began a new journey. His journey would lead to completeness: the completeness of God's plan to reunite us with Him and to propel us into a life that has meaning, value, love, fullness, freedom, and wholeness. Just as Jesus stepped out of the wilderness and into divine purpose, I've discovered so, too, can we. This book is a record of my personal discovery.

In 2010, God first began to stir me to write a book but I didn't know where or even how to begin. Fast forward to 2016 and I was still questioning this call. Thoughts filled my head. *You? Just a nobody who has no idea how to put a book together? What are you thinking? There is no way any publisher will want to look at, let alone publish a book by you! How will you word it, what will you use? You don't even know how to write an introduction, and that's not even the book yet!* The voices were relentless. But I couldn't shake the Holy Spirit's stirring. Deep within me came a heavy, yet loving burden to write a book through which the Spirit can lead and guide people into freedom and wholeness, just as He did for me.

I spent decades stuck in my own wilderness, and I knew that to find its end, I needed to face it. If I did not face the wilderness, I would never be able to step into the next season, or live in the peace and freedom God intended for me.

Our feelings, thoughts, actions, reactions and the decisions we make, are all determined by choices. We often base our choices on our experiences. Those experiences could be the result of someone else's choices, or our own.

How funny that sounds, even as I write it, but that's how we get entangled in this journey we call life. Each day we live with past choices, and each day brings its own new set of circumstances requiring more choices. Some choices create more entanglement, while others loosen us from the bondage of our past and forge a better future. I have learnt and am still learning to make choices that set me free and determine a better future. So, I choose to share my journey with you, a journey that will forever be in the process of growing.

To move ahead in my life, I had to be willing to look back and work through how past choices—my own and others—had affected and influenced me. This process was hard because it was easier for me to pretend most things never happened. When I first began to face my past, I instinctively blamed others. It's what we do as humans, put the blame on other people or things. We go through life thinking this is normal, but it's not normal or healthy. Blaming leads to anger which leads to resentment and even revenge.

For me, learning to respond differently to people and situations happened gradually. Getting started was the hardest part, but as the process unfolded it made more sense. The missing and broken pieces of my life began to be replaced, and I became freer as I allowed God to reshape me.

Life was never promised to be easy. But we can choose to make it the best that it can be by allowing ourselves to be shaped not by our own or others' choices, but by God's. 'God's choices' might sound rather off-putting, but I have come to learn that His choices or ways are truly as He says—for our good. His thoughts towards us are ones of peace and not of evil, intended to give us a future and a hope. He is a just God, but He is also so loving.

Most likely, your journey will not look the same as mine. We humans can never totally identify with another person's path; we can only relate or sympathize. But there is someone who fully understands us—better than we understand ourselves—and who can relate to each and every one of us: God. God alone gives us the strength and power to make the necessary choices and changes that enable us to step onto the new path He has for us—a path where we live out the calling of God, experiencing the completeness of what Jesus achieved and the fullness of what God purposed for us. Jesus has already made this possible. He promised that when He returned to heaven, we would do far greater works than He did! If we will be willing to shift our thinking to line up with God's, this is what we will achieve through Christ.

As you walk through these pages with me, my prayer is that God reveals Himself, His way, and His love to you, and that you will find the path that leads to the end of your wilderness so that you too can begin to look ahead with hope and determination.

PREFACE

I am a Caucasian woman, born and raised in Harare, the capital city of Zimbabwe. The main language spoken in Zimbabwe is English, but there are also a few other official languages; the one I learnt was Shona. I come from a family of eight children. We are a complex family, with four half siblings older than me, one biological sister, named Mickey, and two step siblings. My four half siblings, Mickey and I, lived with Mom and Dad in a standard three-bedroom house in a lower socioeconomic suburb in Harare. My dad was paying a mortgage on the house, making him the property owner.

On properties in Zimbabwe, besides the main house are smaller living quarters where hired gardeners and maids will most often reside. Most families, despite ethnicity and economic status, have a gardener, house maid and a child minder if required, who are all paid wages—they most certainly are not slaves, as is a common misconception. As an example, the child minder I hired when I became a mother had a child of her own, and so she hired a child minder for her child. In Zimbabwe, having a house maid, child minder or gardener does not represent wealth; this is also a common misconception. My dad was an engineer, my mom was a stay-at-home mother but after their divorce worked in administration positions. Mom had a couple of boyfriends after that. In my early teenage years, she married Kevan, who worked as a mechanic.

I was not raised in a Christian home. Mom and Dad knew of God and were familiar with parts of the Bible but never practiced life as Christians. Life was and still is difficult in Zimbabwe as there is no government assistance of any kind, not even for health care or schooling. Hard work is a prerequisite to survival in Zimbabwe. Due to the poverty, there was a lot of criminal activity in the country making safety a large problem for all races. I grew up with so much dysfunction in my immediate family; confusion, abuse and chaos. It wasn't until later in life as I began walking with God and then moved to Australia to build a new future, that I eventually found peace. This is my story.

CHAPTER ONE

The Lord has appeared of old to me, saying: "Yes, I have loved you with an everlasting love; Therefore with lovingkindness I have drawn you." Jeremiah 31 v 3

I don't really have memories before the age of four or five years old. When I first began to look back over my life, I could only remember small snippets—like Mom's constant presence in the kitchen, buttering slices of bread and wrapping them up in cling wrap for school lunches. I was always amazed at how she got the margarine to make perfect waved patterns on the butter knife as she ran the knife across the margarine then smoothed it over the bread. Oh, and the bread! I remember watching her knead the bread dough and thinking I was glad I wasn't the dough! When she finished kneading, she placed the dough on trays, covered it with a cloth, then put it in the warm sun to rise before baking. The spot in the sun was on the roof of a little building near our garage. Mom said she put it there so the dogs couldn't get to it, but I think it was to prevent us little ones getting to it first!

Back then, I didn't have a care in the world. Mom was my hero. I looked up to her and wanted to be just like her someday. But I could barely recall any time with my dad. My only memory is how we stood in a line at the back door behind Mom and took turns to greet Dad when he arrived home from work each day. I briefly saw him again later when he was in the kitchen making his nightly coffee and we had to say good night. That was the extent of my recollections of him when I first looked back.

Finally, the memories flooded back, bringing with them many tears.

They were so painful that sometimes I could only deal with one or two at a time.

◆ ◆ ◆

I was a little older now, around seven, and we were all sitting in the lounge listening to Mom and Dad arguing on the other side of the house. We closed the glass sliding doors and every other door between the lounge and their room in an attempt to block out the ugly noise. Suddenly the doors opened and our parents stood looking at us. They asked each of us in turn who we wanted to live with. I looked at my siblings, not even hearing what they said, and when it got to me, I responded, "You both," still confused with what was happening.

Life changed forever that day as they explained as simply as they could that they were separating, and we had to decide who we wanted to live with. When Dad and Mom walked into the bedroom, Mickey and I followed them. My sister and I stood there holding hands and crying. I was so scared. Dad was weeping too, and from where he sat on the bed, he wrapped his arms around us. The room seemed so dark. Knowing they wanted an answer of who we will stay with and the four other siblings were staying with Mom, I whispered, "I will stay with Mom," hoping that no one really heard.

Dad moved a bed into the loungeroom and that's where he slept for a short time. Then one day we watched him load all his things into his truck (known as a Ute in Australia) and drive out. That was the day my heart broke. I felt as if it was all my fault. Nothing seemed to go right from there, and life changed dramatically.

Mom got a job, made friends and began going out in the evenings. Sometimes she went out at night with my older siblings too. With no other family nearby, it was a lonely time. After a while one sibling stayed around more when we were home, rather than going out with Mom. He was fun and made us laugh when really there was nothing worth laughing about. But it still wasn't the same as it was before.

As Mom now had to work to provide for us, she hired the wife of our gardener, who lived on the premises with us, as a child minder. Louise had occasionally cleaned our house, but now she took on the role of looking after Mickey and me, the two youngest children. I now know she was placed in our home by God. She loved us endlessly and prayed for us without ceasing. She was always there for us, so much so we began calling her, *Amai,* meaning mother in Shona. We also became close to her children. She began taking us to her church because she wouldn't leave us home alone when everyone was gone at night. That's when we saw God's love in action and felt Him drawing us to Himself.

The people at the church seemed to love God wholeheartedly, always seeking Him out and studying His Word. Because of what I witnessed there, I chose to give my life to Jesus. The Bibles in their church were written in the Shona language, and we wanted to read them, so we soon learnt Shona quite well. Amai's children taught us Shona, and as best we could at our young ages, we taught them English. Reading God's Word gave me a hope inside that I couldn't explain. I needed something because the hurt was so big and only seemed to get bigger.

◆ ◆ ◆

Two years after Mom and Dad's separation, their divorce went through. In that time, we very seldom saw Dad, and when we did, he and Mom were always yelling at each other. Dad had grown angry and bitter, which we got most of the blame for, and Mom was rarely around. At home, things got progressively worse. First the electricity was cut off, then the water, and there was seldom enough food in the house. We went next door to ask for water to put in a tin bath in the sun until it warmed up slightly for our bath. Afterwards, we rubbed Vaseline over our bodies to keep as much body heat in as possible.

I remember feeling so hungry I was shaking inside and out. My stomach was so sore I thought it was eating me, and I could barely move to get to the toilet. Amai taught us which leaves to pick off certain bushes that were good to eat, and we did that often. We ate locusts and Mopani worms roasted over the fire. They actually tasted pretty good. Amai roasted sugar on a spoon and put it into hot water so we had something warm to drink on cold days. Most nights we slept on the floor in Amai's quarters, huddled up under a blanket to keep warm. When Mom got home, she woke us up and took us into the main house to our beds.

One day Amai tried to talk to Mom about the situation at the house and the effect on us kids, but she must have felt Mom brushed it off, so she talked to Dad, which didn't go down well. Dad decided to use Amai as a witness in court to fight for custody of my sister and me. Mom was angry and felt betrayed, so she told Amai to leave the property. We never got to say goodbye to her or her husband and kids.

With no child minder, two of my older siblings were now left to mind us after school which was horrible. There was a lot of anger all the time, and again I felt it was my fault. That feeling was constantly reinforced because every day I had to write two or three pages of lines for them saying, "I will listen" or "I will not answer back," and they often gave me a smack. Without Amai there, and with the custody battle still on going, Mom was around more at night and on weekends, but that meant going to the places she went, often waiting while she spent time with her boyfriend and friends. The custody battle went on longer than expected but Mom kept custody in the end and Dad got visitation rights for some weekends and part of the school holidays.

Not long after the divorce, my older siblings began moving out of home. I cried on the veranda as I watched the first of my siblings drive out the gate in Dad's vehicle. I felt like I had just lost another person and wondered when the nightmare would end.

With the divorce finalised, we all seemed to get on with what we had to. Mickey and I were inseparable. Dad was supposed to have us on certain weekends. Often, we sat and waited to be collected, and he didn't show up. On the weekends when he did pick us up, we would not do too much. On Friday nights he took us for a pub dinner, and on Sunday mornings we had breakfast at Wimpy, which is similar to McDonald's. Those were highlights I looked forward to. But much of our time together was spent reliving the past—a past Dad struggled with. I was often told that things were my fault because I had chosen not to live with him, or that I was just like my mother. He would sit there crying, and it tore me apart.

I had a deep hope that Mom and Dad would get back together after Mom and her boyfriend broke up. But then Mom met someone else, and they started a relationship. At first us kids never knew, but then we figured it out because we visited his place more frequently, and he often came to ours and stayed late. This realisation made us all angry. We spoke to Mom, but as she was happy, the situation was not about to change.

At this point, two more older siblings decided to move out of home. Mickey and I found out our siblings had left when we got home from school to find a chocolate bunny with a goodbye-note they had left for us in our clothes cupboard. The note said they didn't know when we would see them again, but that they loved us. It was another blow.

When Dad found out that Mom's new boyfriend Kevan was now living with us, along with his two children (growing my family of siblings even further), he was hurt and angry. There were certain conditions in the divorce settlement with regards to us staying in the house, and he felt these had been broken. According to the legal contract, we had to move out.

In Zimbabwe, there is no government assistance for anything, and so, every day, my sister and I walked to and from school, as Mom never got her licence and couldn't afford public transport. One day we arrived home from school to find Mom and her boyfriend loading a truck with the last of the furniture. We were told to get in the car, and were whisked off. We arrived at a nice new house and were told this is where we now lived.

We hadn't had our usual visits with Dad for a while. There was always a lot of anger between Mom and Dad, and between Kevan and his ex-wife, who was regularly at our house, and we heard it all. In all this anger, Mom told me that if Mickey and I ever saw Dad, we had to run away and hide. Since the custody decision, I had been made to believe that Dad would take us to South Africa and we would never see Mom again. I got so scared when we walked home from school that I watched everything in case we needed to hide, yet deep inside I still wanted to see Dad and know he was okay.

Then, during lunch break one day in my last year at primary school, I saw Dad's vehicle parked outside the school fence. I ran towards him, figuring the fence between us would keep me safe. Dad came up and started crying and telling me he loved us. That afternoon I had things to deliver to the office for the teachers as I was a school Prefect. As I approached the office, I saw Dad talking to the headmaster, who raised his hand to shoo me away. When Dad turned and saw he was motioning to me, he called out to me. I wanted to talk to him, so I walked towards them. But unbeknown to me, the headmaster had been told that Dad was not allowed near us, so he grabbed my arm and pushed me into the staff toilet. This enraged Dad, who in turn ran at the headmaster and pushed him across the desk while shouting at him. Peeping through the toilet door, I saw it all unfolding. I was scared and felt guilty, believing this was again my fault because I did not go away when the headmaster signalled me to. I ran to my sister's class to get her and raced home, taking a new path to avoid anyone catching up with us.

◆ ◆ ◆

It wasn't only the conflict between my parents that was unsettling for me. Things constantly happened around me that robbed me of any sense of security.

One year, a smart-looking car with dark-tinted windows regularly parked outside the school. Everyone was always scared because it looked weird, and we had heard of kids being kidnapped. Tragically, one day my friend's sister was walking home and was kidnapped by someone in that very car, not far from the school gate. She was never seen again. This frightened me, as we always walked home. One day while walking home with Mickey, an army vehicle with soldiers on the back pulled up, and some of them jumped out and chased us. We were so terrified we ran and hid in a water drainpipe. My fear kept growing.

At home, it was no better. Thieves frequently broke into our property, and we could see them through the bedroom window. This scared me, especially because we lived in a house that had no electricity. I always felt that

I couldn't sleep in case someone broke in and kidnapped us or worse, and when I did sleep, I often had nightmares. Mickey and I shared a bedroom and always sat at the window watching for people climbing over the fence or any other suspicious behaviour outside for hours before we could sleep.

But I was also living a waking nightmare. On numerous occasions from the time of my parents' separation, I was the victim of sexual abuse. It confused me. I didn't know what it was or why it was happening to me, especially as I knew some of the abusers well and cared about them. This went on for a long time, but as I was being threatened, I kept it hidden. I was petrified, especially being so young. During that time, all I felt I had was Mickey, Amai, her kids, and the Bible—all of which I clung to. But when Amai left, I felt I had no one, and we had no more church either.

One day after being abused, a family member saw me trying to clean myself. They questioned me repeatedly, and eventually I explained what was happening to me. That day one of my abusers got badly beaten, which only increased my fear. I was told never to say a thing about the situation, which made me believe I had done something to make it happen. I felt lost, confused, and alone. All I could do was read the Bible, even though I didn't understand much. I often just read the same things over and over, and I began writing poems and prayers as I felt I had no one to talk to. When I read and wrote I felt a peace deep inside. Even though I never understood exactly what it all meant, it was like God was still right there.

By now, all I knew was fear. I knew so little good, and the bad drowned out any good that did exist. I learnt that I couldn't trust males and that I had no protection from others, not even from my immediate family, so I had to protect myself and my younger siblings. I was afraid of people who were drunk, of soldiers and strangers, and of doing most things. I felt I had to pay a lot of attention to everything in case I missed a sign of something about to go wrong. I believed that I was not loved and was unworthy of being loved because so many things were my fault. I believed I would never amount to anything in life and was not capable of anything good or positive. I remember feeling I must have been such a bad person, even so young, to have had so many things go wrong. It was as though it was my punishment for being bad. These are just a few of the many lies I believed. It's amazing what children take on and 'wear'.

As I grew up, I had many questions about what was happening to me. Simple questions like, 'Why me?' and 'What did I do to deserve this?' But there was no one to talk to or ask, so I ignored them and believed they were unimportant. Back then, I pushed them away from my thoughts, but they started to resurface in the latter part of my teenage years. Then it was harder to push aside the questions; I needed to make sense of things more. It was always at night, after I climbed into bed, that my mind started to run through the questions I had filed away years before.

All I could see and remember was the sadness, hurt, fear, negativity, and loneliness. Looking back made me angry, and I had so many questions, but it was in asking them that I started to learn who I truly was.

◆ ◆ ◆

My questions were confronting. As a young child, I observed other children at school who all seemed so happy and unafraid—the total opposite of how I felt. *Was their home-life better than mine? Or was I just miserable with my life for no good reason?* When I heard others talk about their family or what they did over the holidays, it caused me to wonder why my family could not do or have the same things.

I never got the opportunity to voice all these questions. Being young had benefits such as the ability to let things disappear into the back of my mind. I kept to myself and did not want to approach people to ask random questions. Part of me would be embarrassed if they asked me about my life, and I preferred to avoid that situation.

Eventually it got harder to ignore the conversations I heard around me at school and to see the lifestyles of other kids without questioning why mine was so unlike theirs. Still preferring to keep my life hidden from others, I went home one day and asked Mom why our lifestyle had to be so different. She explained how sometimes it just is that way in life. God wrote our story and that was how He wrote it. After that, when the questions arose, I tried to tell myself that it was just how it was meant to be, that there was no need to fight it. But it didn't work. The need to fight only got stronger, and the questions became increasingly harder to ignore and push away.

I spent most of my time alone, trying to process my questions, my situations, me. I only felt that I could cope with my life when I was spending time with God, so that was where I chose to stay. Being alone in the world was a burden, but it was the only way I felt safe. I knew God saw all the things happening around me and within me, but sometimes I wished God couldn't see into me, as some of my thoughts and ideas were very far from those I wanted to show anyone—human or Spirit. I always felt I was walking around with a huge cement block on my head and shoulders, and it cast a cold damp shadow that caused mould to grow all over me. I was convinced this was my God-given burden to carry. How far from the truth that was, but it took me a long time to work that out and to accept the truth—the truth that God wanted me to be made complete, and that He had a good future for me.

The older I got and the more I experienced, the more relentless my questions became. It wasn't just the unanswered ones of the past. New questions buzzed through my mind: *Why was I in this family specifically? Why was I given up on? Why wasn't I protected? Why wasn't I good enough or worthy? Why wasn't I believed? Would I ever feel happy and joyful? Would I be successful or spend my life struggling? Was that really my destiny for life on earth? When would I be safe?*

I couldn't seem to push it all away anymore, and deep inside I really did not want to. I just wanted the heaviness and the questions to disappear. The cement block felt heavier and colder. It stirred so many emotions, which made it feel harder to process. Inside, I was sure that at some point, I was going to explode. My mind was like a chaotic highway, with no set direction or control. But at the same time, there was a growing desire to be 'normal' and an awareness of the need to be free. I recognised that the only time I did not see myself as worthless, unlovable, and as having no real purpose, was when my mind and heart were sharing time with God. I developed a deep love and desire for Him. He was my everything.

It was in those times with God, that I experienced His peace and the assurance of His love for me. He patiently and compassionately showed me why all the questions needed answers, teaching me to trust Him and asking me to be willing to let the questions come up and the answers be revealed. This was not easy. Most times I would rather have hidden away. But I found that only certain questions came up repeatedly, even though I had many running through my mind. I learnt these were the ones I needed to work with. God addressed specific questions at different times, never taking me through them all at once. The truth is, God knows what we can handle and when we need to deal with issues. As I came to understand this, I was more able to believe and hold to the truth that God does have a good plan for me.

◆ ◆ ◆

I asked God why He was bringing all these memories back when all I wanted was to wipe them from my mind as though they never happened. I believed I was better off forgetting, but the Holy Spirit stirred me. He revealed that when I push things away, it meant I hadn't faced them nor forgiven, therefore I was living a lie and would never be free. I slowly learnt to begin working with the questions to find the answers.

As I lay in the darkness of my room, while everyone else was sleeping, the Holy Spirit would often drop Bible verses into my thoughts. I would grab a pen and paper, put my head through the curtain to use the moonlight, and write them down. The next day I would read through the verses, then lay in bed that night and ask God what He wanted me to know.

I realised God's Word was alive, and it made me alive. It spoke so clearly to my innermost being that I couldn't ignore it. I knew that God had me, even though the 'Whys?' of my journey were still unclear. I became convicted that to find the truth, I needed to face my past and to forgive. Over the years, I had carried responsibility for all that happened, heaping blame upon myself. I believed it was my fault things went wrong—a lie that was reinforced by what was said to me and by the way I was treated. This lie was consuming me, and I needed to unravel it. I wasn't looking forward to the process, but believing God had me, I decided to push through with it.

◆ ◆ ◆

One of my first questions to God was, "Why, if You loved me, did You let these things happen to me? Why didn't You protect me and prevent it all?"

As the Holy Spirit led me, memories flooded back. I remembered as a little girl, going to a church down the road with Mom. Mom was a nominal believer and occasionally took us to the Anglican or Catholic Church, so God had a little access in my early years. God showed me, through His leading and Word, that He is a gentleman and is not forceful. He works in us as much as we allow Him to. As a child, I didn't know that, and sadly Mom didn't either. She didn't see that she was limiting God's access to our lives.

Being a Christian doesn't mean we will never face trials. If Mom had been in a vibrant relationship with God, giving Him full access to everything, I might still have had a difficult life. But no matter what happened, I would have been able to deal with things and myself better. Mom would have too. It took much longer than it might have for me to see God's plans for good in my life.

As the Holy Spirit helped me revisit the past, I learnt more about God and His Word, more about life in this broken world, and more about people and myself. I finally understood that God never wanted me to experience the pain I had. I saw that things happened because we are born into a world of sin with the element of sin in us, a world in which we have choices. And no, we don't deliberately choose for bad to happen, but every choice has a consequence be it positive or negative. Some consequences are immediate, others take effect later, and some have prolonged repercussions. All affect us and others in some way. Even if we don't realise it, choices are one of the most powerful aspects of our lives.

With my eyes opening to the truth, I could see that when Mom deviated from her walk with God, God provided Amai. Amai was God's seed in my life and a well planted one at that! Now that I see her part in our lives, I thank God for her over and over. There was even a brief time where Mom came to Amai's church and really enjoyed it. We learnt years later that Amai also had an impact on Mom's life. God used the little access He had to full advantage.

Feeling that my questions about God were being answered, or at least now it was making some sense, I started to ask questions about the people in my life and their choices for and with me, questions like: *Why did my mom give up on me? Why didn't my mom love me or protect me? Why didn't my mom ever believe me? Why did my dad leave us waiting for him so many times? Why did he blame me? Why didn't he play an important role in my life, love me or protect me or provide for me? Why didn't he choose to be there for me?*

The answers to these questions didn't always come straight away. Some of them came years later. Like I said, I never got all the answers at once. God knew what I needed and when.

◆ ◆ ◆

During this process I learnt I could actually have a conversation with God through the Holy Spirit as if He were sitting right in front of me. Some days I couldn't pray through the tears and could only write to God. Other times I felt so much anger that I wrestled with God in prayer, especially with the tone of my voice. I wanted to yell at Him but thought we were never to yell at God. One day when I did, I thought I'd blown it, but God used that moment to reveal that nothing I did could change His love for me. He caused me to understand that I wasn't just having a screaming match but building a relationship, and He saw the truth in my heart. He knew my reactions were not the actual posture of my heart; my true emotions were obscured by all the hurt and anger. I was constantly reminded that He knows me deeper and better than I know myself, something He still reminds me of to this day. My eyes were opened to a Love so indescribable yet so real.

But even as I was awakening to God's love, I struggled deeply, believing all that happened to me was a punishment for what I did wrong. For a while I went quiet, not even praying. A numbness settled over me, and I didn't know what I should say or do. It all felt too much. I wondered what else was ahead and how I could face it. At this point I couldn't even bring myself to read the Bible. But God says in His Word that what He starts He will finish, so I knew He was still working in me even if I couldn't hear Him, or if I struggled to read and pray. Whenever I wanted to give up, something inside kept drawing me back. I didn't understand it, but I knew there was something there.

The questions continued to run through my head with not many answers, but then I would feel more memories start to come up. Memories that I had not recollected before. Not all of them were hurtful either. Something was changing! It may not have been big, but even this small change gave me hope and the courage to keep going.

STEP OUT OF THE WILDERNESS

Do you have questions of your own? No matter what they are, write them down starting from the first ones that come to mind. It doesn't matter if it's one, twenty or more. How comfortable are you with asking God questions? If you are uncomfortable, why is this? If you've been holding your questions back, bring the list you have written to God and ask Him. Pray over your list and thank the Holy Spirit that He will reveal the answers as you are ready.

CHAPTER TWO

Likewise, the Spirit also helps in our weaknesses. For we do not know what we should pray for as we ought, but the Spirit Himself makes intercession for us with groanings which cannot be uttered.
Romans 8 v 26

As a teenager I felt a lot older than I was, and I didn't like it. Already I had taken on responsibilities a child shouldn't have to assume, like how school fees would be paid. At the age of twelve, I got a job sorting out policies for funerals at a funeral company, just to help pay the fees. In a way I reasoned with myself that if I refused to take on the responsibilities, then us kids would keep struggling. I never wanted anyone to feel the loneliness and worthlessness that I felt, and I thought that if I did my job well, my siblings would feel loved and treasured.

But just as my fear had kept growing, so, too, did my sense of responsibility. Soon it went far beyond just my siblings, who I often looked after, and extended to other relatives who shared our home from time to time. When my older sister moved in with her new baby and we had to share a room, I began to feel responsible for the baby. When I discovered one of my brothers sneaking in one night and found out he had been abandoned and was sleeping on the streets, my heart broke. Yet again a sense of responsibility arose within me, and I would leave leftover food and a blanket outside my bedroom window for him at night.

One source of normalcy for me was our neighbours. It was their house I had run to the day I raced home after the conflict between my dad and the headmaster, and the father had protected Mickey and I from our arguing parents. Something about that action spoke to me. In my early teens, their son and I hit it off, and we dated for a few years until I was almost fifteen. But as our relationship progressed, it became another source of pressure.

One day my boyfriend told me he knew I wasn't a virgin and questioned why I kept saying no to having sex with him. He gave me an ultimatum. I was so angry. I had never shared with him that I had been abused, and that this was the reason for not being a virgin. Heavy-hearted, I decided that it was best I did what he wanted.

Everything changed after that. He began saying harsh things to me and about me. He had never been like that before, and it hurt deeply. Eventually he ended our relationship. I can't even remember all his reasons, except for the one about me not wanting to sleep with him again and me being totally useless at it. "You were like sleeping with a bag of potatoes," he said. Once again, I blamed myself, convinced that if I had not slept with him or not hated it so much, then he would not have been so mean to me. By this point in my life, I had made the choice to withdraw if I was hurting. I would become quiet and just get on with the things that needed to be done. I wanted to keep busy and focus on others, especially my family, rather than myself.

◆ ◆ ◆

School offered no respite from the pressures of my home life. Being the only Caucasian pupil in my high school, I experienced a lot of bullying, especially by the boys. There were a few girls I thought were friends, but the friendships seemed to fade. I presumed it was because I wasn't allowed to go around to their houses or hang out with them after school. I learnt to keep to myself, knowing that in a few years Mickey would join me there.

At one point I got one of my brothers to come into the school hoping to get him to warn the bullies off. He was a bodybuilder and wasn't the smallest man, but that never worried the bullies. He told me I had to learn to protect myself, so he hung up a huge bag filled with sand and taught me to punch. Just the size of his arms scared me enough to smack that bag with all I had, even if it meant starting with a short run up and punching just enough to get it to move. Oh my, I can see it as I write it, and it brings a smile to my face as I realise how funny it must have looked.

◆ ◆ ◆

Another cause of trouble at school were the fees. Finances were always short and even with my job at the funeral home, my term's school fees were never paid on time. This resulted in being called up on stage in front of the entire school at assemblies and being told that, as long as our fees were not paid, we were not allowed at school. I would go home immediately, talk to my mom and stepdad that night, and beg them to pay the fees, which often took a few days to happen. Embarrassed does not begin to explain how I felt every time it happened, and I'm sure being poor and publicly shamed also fueled all the bullying.

Our financial situation got progressively worse and we had to move again, something that happened often due to bad financial choices. We ended up in a little house that was in a bad area, and I can remember being so scared every day I walked home. I hated the house. It wasn't only that it was in a bad area, the move felt tied into my relationship ending and I was being sexually harassed. This wasn't anything new, it had been happening before we moved, but in this dreadful house, it seemed to escalate. What had started out as forced passionate kisses soon progressed to a 'feeling session' under the guise of play wrestling. I stopped the playing and kept my distance as much as I could, which I would then be yelled at for.

After we moved, some family members began trying to bribe me to just allow them to do what they wanted. I would take off and lock myself away in my room. *Why was I always a male's target?* I didn't understand. I was so terrified that I used to sleep with my bedroom locked. I would take the key out of the door and place a lock block into the keyhole so no-one could use another key to get in, as attempting to get in my room was a habitual occurrence. I didn't want Mom to think I was doing something to invite the abuse.

I remember it being a very bright sunny day when I decided to confide in one of my sisters. I thought if I told her what was happening, she could help me tell Mom. I was told not to worry—she would talk to Mom.

At this time, unknown to me, one night Mom came down the passage to get some water, when she witnessed an attempt by one of my family members. He was naked and trying to get into my bedroom. When she asked what he was doing, he said he was sleepy and thought he was in another room. Mom believed him at first.

After some time and unsure if Mom had been spoken to about my situation, and sexual harassing, I decided to confide in another person, who decided to go to lawyers to ensure that it didn't continue happening to me or others. I can assure you the night the lawyer's letter arrived was not very pleasant, especially since my name was clearly mentioned.

We only lived in that house for a short time before we had to move again. I hoped this would be a good thing and was quietly expecting things to improve. But it turned out to be just another in a long line of moves that never brought any real change.

◆ ◆ ◆

In the midst of all the upheaval of my teen years, a boy (who I later discovered was the boyfriend of one of my sisters) began to take an interest in me. After my breakup with the boy next door, he told me it was the boy's loss, as I was beautiful, and that if I was older, he would date me. Having always felt 'less than', his compliments bolstered my confidence and I soon fell head over heels in love with him. I wrote how I was feeling about this guy in my diary—something I later learnt was a big mistake.

Often when I walked home from school, I would go past the shopping centre where I knew he would be, to chat with him. He told me he was single again, that he loved me and was waiting for me to turn eighteen years old, which was almost three years away. I clung to his words. Then one night my sister came to visit. When she arrived, he was at her side, and they told us they were engaged. I remember the night so clearly. My heart broke and I felt like I wanted to die. He had told me how he loved me and was waiting for me, yet now he was engaged to my sister?! I hid in the garden in the darkest area I could find and wept for what felt like years. When my stepdad, Kevan, eventually found me, he told me to come inside, so I gathered myself and mustered up the courage to tell Mom that I had fallen in love with my sister's now fiancé, and told her all the things he had told me. I thought I was doing the right thing by telling Mom everything. But once again, I was wrong.

When we had to move again and my sister, her fiancé and little family moved with us, it just about killed me emotionally. Before long, her fiancé started to tell me that he was in love with me, and this was the only way he could be close and see me. I believed him and once again confided my hopes and feelings in my diary. My diary felt like the only place where I could be honest about all the things that had happened to me. And then, one day my sister read my diary, unknown to me. After she finished reading it a huge unpleasant argument broke out between us. She was more than angry with me and went directly to my mother. When she too had read it, they decided to call a meeting.

Many of the adults mentioned in the pages of my diary came. They all assembled with Mom in our dining room and denied everything I had documented in my diary. It was at that point that I was called into the room, where I was told in front of everyone, that I had lied about the sexual harassment and that I was lying about my sister's fiancé. I was accused of being jealous and called many hurtful and offensive names by people who should have been looking out for me. But one of the hardest things to process was that I was told I must burn my diary. It was a lot to take in as a young adult, I tell you, especially because I had been truthful. In that moment, I decided I would never tell anyone anything again.

Days after the meeting, my sister's fiancé tried to make excuses for what had happened, telling me he had to deny everything but that he still loved me. Incredibly, I believed him! Out of my desperation to be loved, I clung to his words. From that point on, he began helping my mom and stepdad out by taking us kids to school so we didn't have to either sit in the back of the open truck, which is allowed in Africa, or walk. When he drove us, he told me that if I wasn't sitting in the front seat next to him in the car, that I had to sit behind him. Most times I would be in the front seat in the morning and he would drop everyone else off first and me last, always telling me how much he loved me when he dropped me off at the school. If we were going anywhere in his car and someone else was in the front seat, he would open the back door behind the driver seat and tell me to sit there. While he was driving, he would slip his arm between the seat and car door to rest his hand on my leg as I sat behind him. His actions made me really believe his words and explanations.

In the midst of all of this, a wonderful lady called Ellen came into my life. Ellen was hired as a child minder for my niece. I believe she was sent by God for that season. Ellen became my closest friend. She loved God with all her heart and because of her, my relationship with God got back on track. She got my focus off my sister's fiancé and constantly told me to read my Bible, often reading it with me. She would tell me that men only wanted to use my body, which I never wanted to believe. But one day, I experienced a situation with my sister's fiancé that caused me to finally understand that all he wanted to do was sleep with me. If I hadn't had Ellen in my life guiding me at the age of fifteen, I'm very sure I would have gone along with what he wanted. Because of Ellen, I woke up to the truth that he didn't really love me, and decided to start keeping my distance from him. But even so, guilt consumed me. In my opinion, I was in the category of an adulteress.

We had to move again a few times, but during these times of moving, my sister experienced a difficult pregnancy and found herself in challenging circumstances. As she was no longer living with us and wasn't able to do much, I went to her place daily to look after her during the pregnancy and help with her little family. I felt like I owed her for my wrongdoings; like I was responsible for her in some way.

◆ ◆ ◆

By now my parents were involved with both the rally club and local fishing clubs. Our weekends were spent either marshalling in rallies, running the canteen and bar at the club where the bike races were, or at fishing competitions. I certainly preferred the weekends involved with the rallies. As the years went by, they took us fishing more, as it was too expensive to continue all the hobbies. These activities allowed us to meet a wide range of people. One person in particular stood out: a young man named Colin.

Colin was friendly, and I felt I could talk to him without being judged or blamed for anything (although I never spoke much about my life). In time, we developed a good friendship. I never thought of him in any other way—I didn't really allow myself to. One of my sisters thought he was gorgeous, and I never wanted to come between them or cause hurt like that again. Besides, I still thought all males were terrible if they were anything other than a friend. But as our friendship grew, I began looking forward to the monthly fishing meeting for the chance to catch up and chat.

Then one year, at the fishing club's Annual General Meeting, one of my siblings decided to lock themselves in a car. I didn't want to call my parents because I knew we would all be in trouble. Some of my other siblings and I were trying to break into the vehicle when Colin saw us and came to find out what we were doing. When I told him, he helped get my sibling out the car, breaking into the car using a clothes hanger. Afterwards, we all sat down outside. At first, we were all just chatting, but then we started playing 'catch' and other such games. It was then that things changed for me.

As we were playing, Colin took my scarf, and when I tried to get it back from him, I grabbed his hand by accident. I felt as if I had been shocked and quickly pulled away. It all happened in seconds. I realised that I felt something when I touched his hand, but not knowing if he had felt anything and not being prepared to ask, I decided to be quiet and keep the friendship as it was. He never acted any differently towards me and I told myself that he wouldn't have been interested in me anyway because I came from a poor family. I never talked to him about our home life but fishing was expensive, and we lived totally beyond our means, going without certain necessities and other things to keep up the appearances.

Everyone at the fishing club could see past the pretence, and we were known as being poor.

Throughout these years I saw very little of Dad. The relationship between us had completely broken down, even though Dad still had visitation rights. By now he was dating a lady who we did not get along with, and she had children that we felt had taken our place in his life. They shared a small flat which meant we couldn't stay over, so we would just visit occasionally.

After a few months, Dad moved back to his house, and the next time we went to visit, he announced that we now had a stepmother—he'd married the woman we disliked a few weeks prior. We were shocked! I remember standing there at the gate in the dark and asking him if he was joking with us. After that we saw less and less of him. My heart was broken, but I convinced myself it was best that way. He never had any idea of what our lives were like anyway; he never asked and never tried to be there, so I figured it was best the way it was, even though I was hurt and angry inside.

The more that went wrong in my life, the more insistent I was on finding answers to the questions I had been able to push away in my younger years. As I lay in bed at night, the thoughts got louder and the longing to understand why bad things kept happening to me intensified. The questions continually bombarded me; I felt like I was sinking.

In an attempt to numb the hopelessness, I began to live in a fantasy world, a world where I was safe, where I was the hero, and where I was happy, loved, important, and most of all, in control of everything going on. When the questions felt too hard to face, I would retreat into this place, replaying the things that happened in my life, except this time they turned out alright and I got to avoid all of the pain and heartache my real life held. It got easier and easier to lock myself away in this dream world, but deep down I knew I could not keep pushing the questions away. I somehow knew, even back then, that I needed to take my questions to God once again, and process them before I got lost in a world I would never find my way out of.

I didn't want to keep getting drawn into my fantasy world; I wanted the weight lifted off me; I wanted to feel free. And so, one day, when I was walking home from school, I asked God to reveal the answers to the questions that were causing me so much pain and confusion.

◆ ◆ ◆

Some of the questions that plagued me the most were about my identity. I scrutinised everything about myself, desperate to be everything that I felt I was not: I wanted to be a good person, I wanted to be successful—which for me meant not being poor anymore. But deep down I felt like such a bad person, like a part of me was dirty. I found myself on my knees before God praying for Him to forgive me, to show me what I did wrong and to help me make things right. I wanted to be better and to do something worthy of Him with my life. I started praying that He would take the blindfolds off my eyes, and clear my mind of the fantasy world I found myself trapped in. It no longer felt like a safe place but a cold, dark maze I could not find my way out of.

It's much easier to blame others and focus on their wrongdoings than it is to truthfully face ourselves. While we might admit what we've done, we can tend to make things sound better than they actually are by justifying them in light of someone else's choices or actions. As God began to remove the blindfolds, I started to realise how big the mountain was that I had to face and eventually move. I realised that the only way forward was for me to take ownership of my actions, which meant I needed to work through events in order to find the truth of what I was responsible for.

I had learnt to manage or cope by focusing on my responsibilities. Keeping busy meant I didn't have to face myself or deal with things that affected me. Little did I realise that at some point, whether I liked it or not, the time would come where I would have no choice but to face myself, and by the time I did, there was a lot buried there. As I've looked back over my life, I've learnt and truly believe that God doesn't want us to wait for healing; He wants to guide us and lead us at that moment, so we can move forward and not be in bondage to the past.

Again the Holy Spirit began to take me back, one situation at a time, bringing to remembrance only the things that I needed to deal with in the moment. It was like the shutters were coming off my eyes. God knew what to deal with and when to deal with it in order to get to the core of my brokenness and bring healing. Now, I can see how God had me all the time, and how deeply He knew me and still knows me. But when we're caught up in the middle of something, we often cannot see it for what it really is, especially when it seems like it is one thing on top of another.

I did my best as a young woman to try and deal with what God was showing me, but once again, I kept assuming all the responsibility and trying to fix things in my own efforts. My mom and dad had told me that we must act on things, that God won't do them for us because God doesn't like lazy people. I realised later how confusing this was, but back then, it influenced a lot of how I processed situations. God does want us to take action, but that action should come from faith and with faith, which in turn comes from a relationship with God, Jesus, and the Holy Spirit. We can do nothing without the Holy Spirit. He is our guide in all things because He knows the Father's heart. And we can't go to the Father unless it's through Jesus Christ. We grow that relationship by prayer, worship, and most importantly, reading the Word, the Bible.

As I was working through the questions that had been plaguing me, I saw just how much this false sense of responsibility had pervaded my life.

There was one question I could never escape: *What did I do so wrong to deserve all of this?* Answering it forced me to see that the deep sense of responsibility I felt went far beyond trying to fix things and protecting the people I loved; it flowed from the belief that I carried the blame for all the things that had gone wrong in my life—even my parents' divorce. For years I thought if I was a better little girl and did everything right, then they would have been happy and stayed together.

One memory in particular stood out. In this memory, Mom and Dad were arguing in the kitchen. Normally they argued in the bedroom, and we were told to stay in the lounge while they 'talked', but this night, they were screaming at each other. I remember running into the bedroom. Mom was standing against the closed door leading to the hallway and Dad was standing in front of her, yelling at her. I remember feeling scared but also like I needed to stop them from arguing, so I grabbed Dad's leg and started pulling his leg hairs as hard as I could, shouting at him to stop. Mickey joined me too. But this only made him yell at Mickey and me. We just sat there hugging one another as we sobbed. I so desperately wanted to find a way to make them love each other and stay together. But I couldn't, and it felt like a failure on my part.

Another instance was the night we were told they were getting divorced. When we had to decide who we were going to live with, choosing Mom made me feel that I broke Dad into a million little pieces. I will never forget the way he cried—I felt I had betrayed him and cast him out to be alone forever. I began to realise why God hadn't allowed me to find answers earlier to my questions regarding my mom and dad: If I had found answers back then, I wouldn't have accepted them because I still blamed myself. I realised at this point, that I accepted their choices and actions because I believed they did it because of what I had done. I felt that I couldn't blame them, I could only blame myself.

I started to see that I had made a decision in my childhood years, that I would do everything and anything I could to make others feel better, no matter what it was. I now started to understand how my choices had affected me, especially from my young adult years. I processed things by asking myself if it would make others feel better? If the answer was yes, then I did it, and if the answer was no, I did not. I began to realise that I applied this to situations with my siblings, family and other people. I had chosen to take on all the pain or blame, and I believed that if I carried all the hurt no one else would be hurt, which meant I would never be at fault again. So, when I was told to do things for my siblings, I did it. When I was told to stay home and cook instead of going to school, I agreed. When I was told that I had to give my bed or bedroom up for others, I would. When I was told to give my earnings to my parents, I handed it over. When I was told that I had to be the responsible one, I was.

I believed that I had learnt how to be strong enough to deal with the hurt and pain indefinitely. What I did not realise back then, was that by doing this, I was actually growing my own pain and I would not be able to hide it indefinitely. I did all of this to make sure I could not be blamed, and had convinced myself that by doing all this, Mom, Dad, and everyone else would feel loved and have no more hurt.

Now God was revealing that my true motive was myself. I didn't even think of forgiving them in those years because my motive was to be able to say to them, *I did it all right, you cannot blame me.* I wanted to be better than them, but really, I wasn't any better by what I was doing. It's being motivated by love that allows us to see past our self, yet when we place ourselves first, we are unable to get ourselves out of the very situation that is entangling and blinding us.

I had often wondered why I ended up in the family I was in. Over time I convinced myself that God had put me in the family He did to be the pillar, the strong one who would fix everything. I drew my sense of worth from this role: I was there to hold it all together. In reality, I was holding nothing together. I did all I could to fix things, but it was all temporary. In truth, all I was really doing was prolonging and building hurt and pain not only in myself, but others too.

I had not learnt that I wasn't responsible for others and that I could not change or make choices for them. They would choose to do what they wanted, and nothing I did could or did change them. You see, as a human I can't touch or reach another human that deeply or in a way that will change them. Only God is able to do that. I learnt that the only person I can change is *me*. Only I have the power to build a relationship with God who will reveal things to me, and then as I choose to work with God in that area, He will remould, repair, free, grow, and guide me. I realised God wanted me with this family, and although I may never understand why, I needed to trust that He had the best planned for me and for them. I began to slowly open up my heart and mind. But even as I experienced a measure of peace that I was in the right family, I wrestled with another question: *Why wasn't I good enough to be loved or believed?*

I just wanted my family to see me as a good person and accept me for me (not that I even knew who that was). I looked at all the support I gave and the things I did and was sure that everyone should have seen me as worth something, as capable and able to be relied on. And that's what they did—everyone came to me with their problems because they knew I would take it on board and run with it to the very end, no matter the cost to me. But my perspective was too skewed for me to see this.

As for me being believed, well, I knew I had always told the truth in a situation, but now I saw that it was others who couldn't or wouldn't face the truth. Even if they believed me, they would never admit it because they too never wanted to be seen as wrong or blamed. I saw that God wanted me to learn to accept what I had done wrong, learn from it, and make a change. He desires that very same thing for each and every person in the world. I realised that as long as I wasn't willing to admit my part, I would not be willing to change, and that would keep me in bondage forever.

An admission didn't mean that I was always in the wrong, but it was a way of acknowledging what had happened and of recognising that I could react in a way that was either going to create a positive effect or a negative effect. The truth is, there are consequences for everything, whether positive or negative, and I had to learn to be led by God and keep in step with the Holy Spirit in order to be successful in this area. I had to find my love and worth in God.

◆ ◆ ◆

My history only revealed bad situations with very few good ones scattered in between. The good were so few, I had to really search my brain to remember them. I wondered if I would ever be happy and safe? I had come to the decision and even accepted that my past was showing me my future: a road of hardships forever. I had convinced myself that God allowed me to go through all these things because He was preparing me for the even harder times I was yet to face in my adult years. You see, without knowing it, I had spoken a destiny into my own life, one that was not very welcoming or comforting, to say the least.

Living in a poor family also contributed to that idea. My parents often told us that we had better understand that 'poor was in our blood'. Mom would say that poor was good because in the Bible it said that it was better to be poor than rich—that the poor would inherit the Kingdom of God and would be closer to God. *Did this mean I would always be poor?* Much later on, I learnt that the meaning of this teaching in Luke was not that everyone had to be poor to be closer to God, rather it meant that when we don't chase after success and all forms of wealth according to the world, but focus on God first, then we will inherit His Kingdom.

When I was growing up, being poor meant to me what it meant to my parents: to have nothing, to struggle for all things, to experience endless hardships, to have to work hard and strive every day for very little, to be used and abused by others, to be seen as nobody in the world, a person who had no view, opinion or ability to impact anyone or achieve anything in this life. Later in life, I realised that was not my destiny nor anyone else's destiny planned by God. I had to get a new way of thinking, a new mindset. I needed to grasp the truth, because while being poor and broken does have the ability to bring people to realise there is a God and to cry out to Him, I have come to learn that it doesn't actually bring us closer to God. Sometimes it can do the opposite.

As we suffered through situations, I found myself questioning why my life was so difficult. I had always been told that the details of our life were written in His book, the 'book of life'. *Why did God write it in the Book of Life that we had to have it hard?* Even when something went right, it was easily forgotten as the next hardship came along. I can remember feeling like God would do a good thing every now and then just to dangle a carrot in front of me, giving me a glimmer of hope so that I would carry on. This caused me to be mad at God. But because God is God, I thought I better accept what He serves. The walls went up between God and me, and what should have been a fulfilling, encouraging, empowering, and satisfying relationship became strained.

When we are always struggling with things, we are not happy. How can we be when we're feeling unsafe and vulnerable? When we have no destiny that is worth holding onto or to look forward to? That is not God's idea of abundant life! I realised that as I had accepted this way of life and believed my future destiny to be as my past was, there was no way I could ever be happy or safe. How could I even genuinely love God? Realistically, I couldn't, because there was always a part of me questioning why a God who is good and says He plans for a future of prosperity and hope for us, gave me all I had faced, with more still to come. That left me doubting God and His Word, leaving very little chance for me to ever trust Him.

I had to learn that my happiness and safety come only from God and that He really does mean what He says. I knew that I still needed to have a reverence for God because of who He is, but I also needed to learn how to truly love. True love means that you put others first, you want to see them smile, you want to make them happy, you want to be with them, you never intentionally hurt or anger them and you never expect anything back in return for anything yet always stay true and honest with them. I realised this could only be done when I knew God's true love for me. You see, His love feeds and equips, and in turn, it can be given out. True love comes with wisdom too, which is very important, and I needed it so I could be sure not to fall into traps in the future.

In between the bigger questions, there were many smaller ones, and they all led me to many hours, days and even months of soul searching. At times I felt like I was not getting anywhere fast and felt frustrated. All these were lessons, lessons of stopping, listening, praying, seeking, and letting go—lessons which enabled me to look back and see the things that God had already started working in me or showing me.

It blows my mind at the patience God has had with me, the way He has known me, the perfect timing He has chosen to bring out the best in me and free me, to refill me with Him, and draw me deeper into a relationship with Him. I often think if I were God and had been watching me, I would have said "too hard" and run the other way, not looking back. But I am so thankful that God only sees us through His eyes, through Jesus, and that He never forgets His plan to be with us, to share with us, to keep us close. He never leaves us for a moment!

STEP OUT OF THE WILDERNESS

Are you carrying a false sense of responsibility for what has happened in your life? Sit with the Holy Spirit awhile. What is He showing you about those situations? What is He inviting you to release and entrust to the Father? Why do you think God doesn't have enough for you? I encourage you to work with the Holy Spirit. You may feel hurt or uncomfortable and even vulnerable, but keep going, no matter the pace you move at.

CHAPTER THREE

As for God, His way is perfect; The word of the Lord is proven; He is a shield to all who trust in Him. For who is God, except the Lord? And who is a rock, except our God? It is God who arms me with strength, and makes my way perfect. He makes my feet like the feet of deer, and sets me on my high places.
Psalm 18 v 30-33

As a child, I desperately wanted to be different from my family. I didn't want to struggle and go without all my life. I wanted to have money—not only for myself but also so I could help others. I'd daydream about buying a house for each of my family members and then the homeless. Then one day I had a vision of a round-shaped shopping mall; I owned the building and shop owners rented it from me. Another time, I had a vision of me standing at a board table with others around it and I was the leader. I didn't fully see it at the time, but God was already starting to plant dreams and hopes in me. I knew I needed to start somewhere if it was all to become a reality, so I set out to find a job.

I was twelve when I started working part-time at a funeral home where a relative also worked. I gave most of the money to my folks to cover school fees, food, rent and so on. My priority was making sure expenses were covered in the house, especially school fees. I was so tired of us children being humiliated at school for the fees not being paid. But even then, I kept a little set aside, enough to buy one item a month for my 'bottom drawer'. My bottom drawer was my pride and joy. Each month I would buy a plate or bowl or spoons or whatever I could afford with what I had kept aside, building up items for the day I moved out of home. The confusing thing was that I was preparing to leave home, yet I was scared to leave. I was scared to leave because I was not sure that my younger siblings would be okay without me there. Nonetheless I kept moving forward, doing everything within my power to secure a better future.

◆ ◆ ◆

When I was sixteen, the time came for me to sit my major exams at high school. The results of these would decide whether I could go to university, and I was determined to pass them with very high marks. I believed I was going to change the course of our family history. But studying was very hard, given my circumstances, and when exam time came, I only passed four out of the nine subjects that I sat exams for. I was devastated.

Throughout my school years I had no support at home or from my teachers. I was constantly being humiliated and bullied, on top of trying to deal with the turmoil of adolescence. No one had ever nurtured or cared for me. None of my parents had taken the time to really communicate with me. They seemed to believe that children had no opinions, and that even if they did, they didn't matter. My feelings seemed to have no value and so I was left to stumble through life, basically just doing what I was told to. Now it was my downfall.

The day I came home from school with the exam results and handed them over, my parents were so angry. They yelled at me and told me that they had wasted all their money on school fees for nothing. I wished I could just stop breathing. My results meant there was no possibility of going to university in the future; I had lost all my dreams and hopes of changing the course of my family history. I felt like I would never be able to do anything worthwhile and I would be stuck working at the funeral home forever.

That week we went to the fishing meeting, where I saw Colin, who proceeded to tell me his exam results. Needless to say, I kept very silent about mine. I decided to start to search for a career that didn't require university qualifications, and thought about being a midwife or air hostess. But I was told I was too short to be an air hostess for a start, and that I needed to learn seven languages in addition to English. To be a midwife was no easier—I needed to find a hospital willing to take me in as a general staff member, then sponsor me to study as a midwife. There was no hospital in Zimbabwe doing this, so I decided to learn accounting. I got the basics from my older sister, who had been taught a few things, and from Mom who was a receptionist and did banking, typing, and debt collection. When someone we knew who had a small business and was looking for someone to do the books gave me a job, I said goodbye to the funeral home and went to work for them.

◆ ◆ ◆

My friendship with Colin had grown significantly. We talked on the phone every few days, had a laugh and cheered each other up, but I still hadn't said anything to him about the feelings I had experienced when I touched his hand months earlier. One day at a fishing meeting, Colin asked me to go to a movie with him. He suggested a Friday night movie in two weeks' time, as he knew I had to get permission from my parents. He had just got his driver's licence and was happy to pick me up. I knew I had to talk to my sister about my feelings for Colin and I was so nervous, but to my surprise, she was very calm and understanding, even though she said it still hurt as she felt every boy she liked, liked me instead.

With everything sorted between my sister and me, I spoke to my parents, who told me in no uncertain terms that the trip to the movies was never going to happen. I said that as I was working, I would keep a little extra of my pay to cover the cost of the movie, thinking they said no because I would be spending money which I would normally give them, but they still would not hear of it. I waited a few days and spoke to them again, and this time a family friend who was at the house suggested that my parents accompany us to the movies. My parents agreed and said that if they came it would work. I didn't understand this, but I called and explained the situation to Colin and he said it was fine.

On the Friday the movie was planned for, there was a funeral which the adults in the family attended. Early evening came around and they hadn't arrived home yet, so I called Mom to ask if they were on their way as we had to get going for the movie? Mom said no, so I said I was still going and hung up. I knew that this was not going to go down very well when I got home. In the end, my parents' friend decided to come in their place. It was a nice evening with Colin, but when I got home, my parents and I got into the biggest argument we'd ever had. I got shoved into the bedroom wall, and for the first time, I screamed back at them. That night was the first time Mom told me she was sorry for letting me down. It meant so much to me, but her apology made my stepdad so mad, he threatened a divorce and drove out the gate. It wasn't until the following morning that he simmered down and came back home.

The following month, Colin invited me to another movie. This time, my mom and stepdad came along. I went in Colin's car, and they followed us in their car and sat four or so rows away from us.

Months later, Mom said that she just knew that Colin and I were going to get married. I laughed, but a few days later Colin called and asked me if I was interested in dating him. I remember saying, "sure", and hanging up after he said, "I will come see you in the next hour." I was standing there speechless when Mom came up and asked who called. I said "Colin." She looked at me and said, "Did he ask you out?" I nodded as she walked away. Well that did not amuse the other adults in the house. Two of the men who lived with us cornered me and told me that they were going to teach me exactly what Colin would expect of me. I screamed, and for the first time Mom came through and intervened.

Colin came over and I told him very little. I was sure he could feel the tension, but he never said a thing. Slowly but surely, after numerous arguments about me dating Colin, I got more determined and stronger in making my own decisions, while still trying to honor each of my parents.

During these years we continued to move regularly. Finding a new house was not always easy, and one time a relative allowed us to move in with them. Living together was rather difficult and there were a lot of arguments, mostly over finances. The best thing I remember about staying with them was the Sunday lunches where we got to eat delicious roasts and puddings. But in time, things got too difficult, and we had to move again.

We moved into numerous houses before a flat my aunt had been living in became available. As it was a small flat, Mickey had to go live with Dad and my stepmother while my other two siblings went to live with their mom and stepdad. I struggled with being separated from them. For some reason I was not allowed to visit Mickey at Dad's house. No one would let me in the gate when I went there. I don't know if Mickey knew I tried to see her, but I didn't want her to think I had abandoned her. One day I got a note from her while I was at work telling me how alone she was, how unhappy she was, and how she wanted to stop living. I was so scared she was going to try and take her life. I spoke to Mom about her coming to live with us.

After many discussions with my parents, Mickey came to live with us again, which made me happy. Although there were a few of us living in the flat by now, for me, the next priority was to get my other younger siblings back home. Every day they were away I was worried about them. We would sometimes visit them on weekends and they would share how difficult it was living there. They were always sad. It always drove my desire to get them back home, close to me. I felt I needed to have them back so I could love them and care for them properly.

The area we lived in was not a very safe one and there was a store that sold alcohol a few metres from the flats—we called them beer halls. One night I heard a woman screaming, a scream that made my blood run cold. I looked out the window, after turning all the lights off so no one from the outside could see me looking through the window. I saw a fight, three men broke beer bottles and were stabbing and cutting another man. It was the worst thing to see, and I could do nothing to help. It made me want to hide away from the world. Then, I thought I saw one of my older siblings at the railway station which was opposite the block of flats and beer hall. I sat there watching, as the person I thought was my brother placed a flattened cardboard box on the ground under the seat and then lay on it. Watching that made me remember how much I wanted to be successful to help people like that live a bit easier.

I watched out that window for hours as the street quietened, then I snuck across to the railway station to see if it was my brother. To my surprise and horror, it was. I gave him a fright as I stood staring at him. He was so dirty, and my heart broke. Yet again, I felt that sense of responsibility. I took him and hid him in a little cupboard under the stairs that led up to the flat we lived in. I snuck food into the cupboard and blankets every night and I hid a key for him to get into the flat during the day to have a wash. At night, he would often snore; it would echo in the passageway up the stairs and I would quickly rush down to wake him to stop the snoring. Then one night, a tenant from one of the other flats found him and I got into trouble again. As he had been found, Mom allowed him to stay in the lounge. He could not stay indefinitely, but at least he had somewhere to sleep, wash, and eat.

Living in the flat meant I was approximately thirteen kilometres from work. My place of work was not in the same direction as my parents' workplaces, so instead of catching a ride with them, I had to walk or take the local transport, which was a minibus also known as an emergency taxi back in Zimbabwe. I avoided the minibuses as often as I could because the drivers were very unsafe. They would cram in nearly double the number of people allowed. In Zimbabwe, in a vehicle, you can have passengers sitting on other passengers' laps or in the open back of a truck. The minibuses were mostly owned by the driver, who used that as a source of income for them and their family, so the more they could get in the vehicle each trip, the better for them. I chose to walk to and from work most days. A few times I was followed, and one night I was robbed. I had just been paid and was not prepared to lose my whole month's salary, as people are only paid monthly in Zimbabwe. That night I chased the man who stole my bag. I recovered it, but looking back, it was not a safe thing to have done. Yet again, God was protecting me.

We had lived in the flat until one of the young men at the fishing club asked my folks if they were interested in renting his house. They agreed to it and we moved. Yet again, it was not a safe area and there were many burglaries. Often, we woke up to the tyres missing from the vehicle or something like that. But the house was much bigger than the flat, so my other younger siblings were able to come back to live with us which made me very happy. Things had been tough, but at least we were together again, and I felt I could love and protect them better now.

◆ ◆ ◆

I got along well with most of the people at work but there was one partner I was always unsure of—as it turned out, for good reason.

It was the start of a week and as I made my way to work, I thought the air felt thin and chilly even though the sun was shining bright and there was not a cloud in the sky. When I arrived at work, I found a pornographic book on my desk. I was against this sort of thing, and presuming one of my bosses had accidentally left it there, I moved it to their desk area and proceeded to get on with my work.

It was sometime in the morning when one of my bosses arrived and asked if I had seen the book he had left on my desk. Thinking he was looking for it, I responded that I had put it on his desk. He then clearly informed me that he had left it there for me to look through. I laughed, thinking he was joking, and continued working. At the end of the day, however, the boss returned to my office and advised me that I needed to look through the book, and if I didn't meet his expectations, I would be dismissed. I went home without the book, but now I was not sure if he was serious or joking, so I tried to put it out of my mind.

At work the next day, just before the morning tea break, my boss came and asked me if I had thought on what he said. I advised him that I was not interested in that sort of thing. He was not impressed with me and made me feel uncomfortable. I should have followed my instincts, which were to get out of the office, but I didn't. He came over, grabbed me, then pinned me to the wall. Holding my arms above my head by my wrists, he ripped open my shirt. I was so scared and shocked, but at that very moment, another boss of mine came in, and when he saw what was happening, he intervened. I was given a jacket to wear to cover me up and told to call someone to pick me up and get out of there. I immediately phoned Colin to come and collect me urgently. I never returned to that workplace. Again, looking back, I see that God protected me by arranging the timing of my other boss' arrival at the office.

Now jobless, I needed work desperately. Thankfully, there was a couple who we fished with who had a bookkeeping company and were looking for someone to do the general bookkeeping, so I went for an interview and they employed me. I worked there for almost a year, until they dismissed me, right before they left to move to Australia. They gave me two reasons for the dismissal. The first was that when they were away from the office, I was not at work. This was not true, but I had no proof I had been there. I had been late to work for two days as I had to go and collect documentation for their visas, but when I tried to explain that they would not listen. The second reason was that I had made an error in one set of data captures. I was told to leave immediately. I was devastated and wept all that afternoon. I felt so humiliated and useless. I questioned whether I knew anything about accounting. It made me feel that mistakes were not acceptable or correctable in accounting.

At this time, Mom worked at a college that offered accounting courses, and when I noticed some brochures there, I decided to enrol and get my accounting qualifications. The whole time, however, I doubted my abilities. Not feeling good enough had eroded my confidence. Looking back, I know I could have achieved higher results had I been more sure of myself. But the constancy of the challenges and abuse I faced had cemented my insecurities and decimated my self-worth.

◆ ◆ ◆

Up to this point in my life I believed that everything that happened was written as part of my life plan, God's plan for me. I had not yet learnt that it wasn't God's plan for me to be abused or humiliated or treated unjustly. I could not understand why deep down I felt that living this way was not right. Sometimes, I thought that feeling these things was wrong and it was just me being selfish! You see, in these later teenage years, with all these situations I had experienced, I had begun feeling and believing that I shouldn't have dreams or even hopes. I felt I was useless, unable to do anything worthy, that I couldn't be loved, that there was no one out there who would protect or provide for me. I felt that the only way to survive was to build walls around my heart, become cheeky and even controlling at times, and do everything myself, never letting others close.

◆ ◆ ◆

As negative situations occur, I believe they leave deep wounds. When the next situation comes along, if we haven't experience healing, it makes the previous wounds bigger and harder to ignore. That's what my life felt like.

In trying to clear my confusions, I found I thought on things a lot, which meant living it all over and over in my head. The more I thought of the situations, the hurts and confusions, I found that I kept coming back to the idea that I must have been the bad one, just as everyone kept saying. After all, I was the common entity in every situation.

I still saw Mom and Dad's divorce as my fault. *Why?* Because I thought I wasn't a good enough daughter. My feelings, even at that very young age, were confirmed with Dad blaming me because I chose to live with Mom, and saying I was just like her. Since that time, Dad had told me this so often that it was deeply embedded in me. And when I saw him weep uncontrollably, it reinforced my belief that I was a bad daughter—I had broken his heart. When I'd sit for hours waiting for Dad to pull up at the gate and pick me up only for him to not show up, it proved to me that I was a burden; I wasn't good enough to be loved by him either.

When Mom had gone out night after night, again I thought it was because I was a bad daughter and she didn't want to be around me. I don't recall ever having any conversations with Mom as she got ready to go out; I just remember sitting there watching her dress up and do her makeup and desperately wanting to ask her to stay home with us, just for the night. But I felt invisible, a burden even. The fact that some of my older siblings would also get ready to go out with Mom further embedded this lie that I was unlovable, and I assumed they all wished I was not there.

When I failed at school and in important exams, and then getting the responses I did, I felt I was wasting my time hoping; I was stupid and incapable of achieving even the basic things required in life so there was no point in dreaming of a better future. I needed to do well in school to get a career and I couldn't even do that. I remember thinking, *Why do I bother studying? I can't remember it and don't understand some of it.* If I asked anyone for help, I would be given a brief explanation about it, and if I didn't understand, I was told that I would never get it. Being shut down when I asked for help taught me not to ask questions. I felt my questions were stupid, because everything should have been easy to understand. But it wasn't easy for me to understand, and it left me feeling stupid.

When I was abused again and again, it only proved to me that I caused these things to happen. I thought, maybe I was flirting and causing men to hurt me like they did, and that I couldn't be loved, only used and mistreated. I believed I was not meant to have feelings, opinions, or dreams, but only be mistreated; that I was only important to a man if I did what he wanted. Being in love with a man who lied to me to try to get what he wanted, told me that no man was trustworthy, just like the father-figures in my life who never showed any care for me.

When I was dismissed from my job, it told me that I made mistakes others didn't, and that if I made any mistake, there was a huge price to pay. It also made me believe that I was useless at accounting, which was hard for me because I had nothing else.

When people talked about me the way they did, it told me that I was not good enough for anyone, that I was built to be alone, that I was unloved and couldn't fit in anywhere. As a result, I felt I had no one to trust or confide in.

Even at school, when the girls did things I disagreed with and I said what I thought, they would tell me off, or if I stood or sat with them, most times they would turn away. They made me feel like they never wanted me around them, like I wasn't good enough to be in their groups or be their friend.

All these things led me to believe that every bad thing that had happened must have been because of me. That what I did must have always been wrong.

The few people who did believe in me and were encouraging me along the way were drowned out by the majority. What God was doing was obscured by the continual hardship. And yet God's Word kept me from giving up, even if I didn't fully see it back then. I just thought I was a strong person and that's why I never gave up. I couldn't see that it made me hard, broken, and alone.

STEP OUT OF THE WILDERNESS

How do you view yourself? Is there a dream God wants to revive that you have lost sight of because of your suffering? Invite the Holy Spirit to show you how you can partner with Him to take a step towards realizing the vision God has given you.

CHAPTER FOUR

Stand fast therefore in the liberty by which Christ has made us free, and do not be entangled again with a yoke of bondage.
Galatians 5 v 1

Colin wasn't like most of the other guys I'd known. The first time he kissed me was a few weekends after we began dating. There was a fishing competition at the lake and after all the weighing in of the fish and socialising, I helped Colin load his belongings into the car he was driving. We closed the boot and I climbed up and sat on it while we chatted about the day's fishing. Colin said that he had better go home as he was on duty at work at 6 a.m. and wanted an early night. It was then that he looked at me and asked if he could kiss me. Even as I think of that moment now, I can remember how it made me feel special and so respected. I smiled and nodded then he leant in and gave me a quick but gentle kiss. I hopped off the boot feeling like I was about to fly, waved, and tried to walk away casually.

When I got home, Colin had left a message for me to call him—which of course, I promptly did! He told me that his parents were going away and asked me over for dinner on Friday. I said yes, hung up, and told my folks that Colin had invited me to dinner at his house on Friday and I had said yes. Their reply was that I couldn't just say yes without clearing it with them first, but then Mom surprised me by saying it was fine and that they would not accompany me. Instead, they would drop me off and pick me up at 10.30 p.m.

Friday came, and we had a lovely dinner together and watched a video. A few weeks went by and he invited me over for dinner again. This time my parents agreed to pick me up around 11.30 p.m. That night, Colin and I ate, then fell asleep while we lay on the couch together watching a movie. We were woken up at 11.35 p.m. by all the hooting from my parents at the gate. The following week we went out to the movies, and after leaving the movie, Colin took me home. We talked for a while at my place, and then he leant over and kissed me in a way he hadn't before. One thing led to another, and we slept with each other that night. I was worried that maybe that was all he wanted and now he had achieved what he wanted, he was going to dump me.

I went into the room I shared with Mickey, trying to be as quiet as I could as I climbed into my bed, but I needn't have worried. She was still awake. She asked me if I had a good night and I said yes. The truth was, I was kicking myself for what had just happened.

For the next two weeks I was quiet, and I didn't hear from Colin either. I was sure that my fears of him getting what he wanted and dumping me had come true. I remembered when we were friends, he shared that a girl had written a letter telling him she wanted to marry him. He had said he wouldn't reply to her letter, he would just ignore her, and that if he didn't want to see a girl again, he would just stop talking to her. Logically to me, it was all adding up and I was sure I had been dumped. In my insecurity, I presumed that Colin had slept with most, if not all, the girls he had dated or been out with, and now I was added to that list.

Three weeks passed, and we had another fishing meeting planned. I didn't really want to go, and believe me, I made a scene about it! But Mom put her foot down and told me we were going. I sulked my way into the car and up the stairs to the meeting room where I sat silently. I mentally worked out Colin's roster from the last time I saw him; I was sure he would be on night duty. He worked for a tobacco processing company, where he was rostered for two weeks on day shift, and two on night shift.

Earlier that evening, when Mickey had asked me why I was not happy about going to the meeting, I told her what had happened and how I had heard nothing from Colin since then. That night, Mickey sat right next to me and held my hand in moral support.

The meeting began, then the door opened and in walked Colin. I still remember what he was wearing: blue boxer shorts, black T-shirt, light coloured socks, and fellies (a Zimbabwean boot). He walked over to his parents' table and sat down. I kept looking down, holding tightly onto Mickey's hand. All I wanted to do was weep. The meeting came to an end and I felt too scared to move from the chair. Colin came over after saying hi to other people and greeted my family, but I never looked up. Then he asked me if I wanted to go for a walk around the field. When I didn't answer, Mickey jabbed me with her elbow. "Sure," I said as I got up, still trying not to look at him.

We walked across the field not saying a word until we reached the only bench there was, and sat down under the streetlight. I didn't know what to say, so I continued to sit there in silence. Colin took my hand and told me he was sorry he had not called before. Then he placed an envelope in my hand. I didn't want to open it as I was sure it was a "Dear Janet" letter, telling me why I wasn't good enough for the relationship. As I slowly opened it, however, I felt a rectangular shaped object. To my surprise, Colin had carved 'I Love You' into a metal plate and painted it. With the gift was a piece of paper he had burnt 'I Love You' into.

I started to cry from relief, but I still couldn't look at him. He took my hand and told me that after we had slept together, he had feelings and emotions about me that he had never felt before and he hadn't called because he didn't know what to say. I told him I thought that he had dumped me and why, and he corrected my thinking about sleeping with other girls.

From that night onwards, we spoke to each other daily and our relationship progressed at a steady rate. By now my folks had come to terms with us dating, but Colin's parents still didn't like me or the fact we were seeing each other, although they still had me over to visit. Colin decided he didn't want to keep processing tobacco, but wanted to go to college and become a tobacco farmer. The college was out of town, which meant we would see much less of each other, but I understood he was trying to build a better future.

At first, I gave my parents money for fuel, and they would take me to visit Colin, as I didn't have my licence. But after a month or so of being at the college, Colin often chose to go out with the guys over seeing me. We would plan a date, and then he would cancel last minute. I heard he was drinking and going out to nightclubs a lot. One night I shared with him what I had been told and asked what was going on. His response was that I was taking our relationship too seriously, and he could do what he wanted. Needless to say, we ended up in an argument. I went back into the flat sobbing and he drove off in a rage. We did not speak for a little while, although it felt like forever.

◆ ◆ ◆

Our relationship continued but was always on tenterhooks. I was somewhat surprised when Colin invited me to join him and his family for their annual Christmas trip to Kariba. His parents were happy with me going, so I spoke to mine and agreed to go. It was my first trip away and my first time visiting Kariba. I was so looking forward to it. I also hoped it would be a chance for Colin and me to get closer and work on repairing our relationship.

We were staying in a little chalet, and Colin and I shared a room with two single beds in it. His parents had us keep the door open—they didn't know we were sexually involved yet. On the first morning when we got up early to go boat fishing, I went to the toilet and Colin went to shower. Now the toilet and shower shared one big room, but each was separately partitioned off. Colin's mom, however, noticed us in there and presumed we were in the shower together. As I walked out from the room, she started screaming at me, telling me I was no good for Colin, that I was misleading him and making him to do things that were wrong. She said that she never wanted me to go on the trip, and that I had ruined the holiday.

Now, I am not a person who wakes up with a big smile on my face and ready to take on the world, let alone take on an argument. I was caught by surprise and replied saying that I was not sure what I had done wrong.

Colin's mom yelled at me, "You were in the shower with Colin," to which I tried to reply, "No, I was in the toilet." But she kept yelling, so I yelled back. I was angry that she had jumped to conclusions and was now screaming at me based on her presumption rather than facts. Colin heard the yelling from the shower and came out. *Great,* I thought. *He will clear it up that we were in separate rooms.* But to my surprise, he yelled at me, saying he had never had a girlfriend who yelled at his mother like I did, and that he would not have that. I was told I was not welcome on the boat for the day.

I stood there in shock with my mouth open so wide that it felt like my bottom jaw was on the cement floor. Colin walked off to the boat with his parents. I was so angry. I didn't even have time to feel hurt. I climbed back into bed for a while and then decided to go sightseeing.

That night was the night before Colin's mom's birthday. When they came back from fishing, everyone was silent. We ate dinner, and I decided that I would leave them alone. I went off in the dark and found some friends who were also in Kariba for Christmas, and we sat talking for a little while. I then sat alone watching the stars and listening to nature. I just needed space.

Unbeknownst to me, Colin had come looking for me. By the time he found me, he was angry, and questioned where I had been in a way that was rather accusatory. We had yet another argument, then went back to the chalet to sleep. When morning came and they were loading the boat, I wished Colin's mom a happy birthday, but got no response so I walked away and went back to the chalet. Colin stayed by the boat for a short while and then came into the chalet. He told me if any girl did not respect his mother, he couldn't date them. He said he was going fishing with his parents and that we were no longer together. I was angry and hurt, but I said nothing and walked away, needing time to process all this.

I made my way to the swimming pool and sat on the bench thinking, *What a great holiday this turned out to be!* Just then, a friend came across and sat next to me. He asked me where Colin was, and I told him he had broken up with me and had gone fishing. A few others arrived at the pool, jumped in, and started to splash me, so I jumped in too. I had not been in the pool long when Colin appeared and asked me what I was doing, to which I replied, "Having fun!" This was the wrong answer! He told me I had to get out the pool, to which I said, "No, you dumped me, remember, so I can do as I choose." He turned away and stormed off. Later, Colin's parents told us how angry they were with us both. I hadn't known that Colin's parents never took him fishing that day, or that Colin had fished along the banks of crocodile-infested water all day. Not wanting to argue anymore, I just walked away.

The next day was New Year's Eve. There was a party about twenty minutes away from where we were staying, which we had planned to go to. Colin's parents were still angry with us and refused to let Colin use the vehicle, but eventually relented. As we drove to the party, Colin told me he had not broken up with me, that I heard wrong and that he simply wanted me to show his parents some respect. We made up and had a good night seeing the New Year in with friends. The next morning, I apologised to his parents for yelling as I should have spoken better, but explained I was not sorry for defending myself, as I had been wrongly judged and wasn't given the chance to explain the situation. The tension eased a bit for the rest of the holiday.

When we got back to Harare, Colin dropped me at home and headed back to his parents' house for the night, where they had a conversation that left Colin feeling that our relationship was wrong. When I went to visit him at the college the following week, he told me he wasn't sure if we were going to work, and that he needed time to think about it. Again, I left all upset, not knowing if he would call me or if I would just never hear from him again. I had handed him my heart by now, and wasn't sure how I would come out the other side of this. I found it hard to accept, as I had fought with my parents to be able to date him, and yet, because of *his* parents, he was ready to dump me.

After a few days, Colin called and said he was coming into town and would like to talk. He told me that he realised he cared for me and did not want to break it off at this point. We never saw a lot of each other over the next few months, but I consoled myself with the fact that we were still dating. When we saw each other, he gave me little letters he had written to me during the time we had been apart. But every time I went to his parents' house, I remained quiet and reserved to ensure I never got into another argument, which meant my relationship with them did not progress. I felt that his parents had already made up their mind about me, and there was nothing I could do to change it.

◆ ◆ ◆

Colin finished college and was offered a job on a tobacco farm about an hour away. This was around the time that I got fired and decided to study accounting. Now that I was at college, Colin would come into town for weekends and stay with his parents. Normally, he would organise to meet all his friends from college at a nightclub, and I would go with him. This was my chance to see him—well, sort of see him. One weekend he came into town for a friend's bachelor party and got very drunk. When he arrived at my house, he wasn't even sure where he was. I was so mad at him. He had to leave early the next morning to coordinate some things on the farm. He got very emotional before he left, which I had never seen before. He said it was because he didn't want to leave me, but I believed it was because he was still drunk and feeling sorry for himself.

That week passed, and the next weekend, I got a ride to the farm with some friends whose boyfriends were working in the same area. On Sunday, when I was saying goodbye, Colin gave me a letter he had written. I packed it in my bag, climbed into the car, and set off home.

When I got home and finished unpacking, I sat down and read the letter. In the letter, Colin wrote that he had thought long and hard, and decided he wanted me to move to the farm to live with him, and to find work there. I didn't take this seriously, and told him that week that my answer was no. I said this because I still felt I could not leave my family, as my pay helped cover the school fees and other bills. I didn't want any of them to go without, or even lose the house, because they didn't have enough money.

When Colin visited again a few weeks later and asked me the same question, I gave the same reply. That weekend Colin told his parents that he had asked me to move in with him. This led to a huge argument, and in the end, Colin told them that he was not going to talk to them again until they had accepted me into the family.

The following weekend Colin was at the dinner table at my place when he told my parents that he really wanted me to move to the farm with him and was asking for their permission. When I think back to that night it all seems so fuzzy, like it played out in slow motion. I was not expecting him to do that, nor had he pre-warned me. I am not sure who answered first, but I remember their first response being, "No, because we need her money."

Colin stood up, never said a word, reversed his car to the door of my room, which led outside, opened the boot, threw my clothes in it and told me to get in the car because we were leaving. By now I was crying. My siblings were sobbing and hugging me, asking me to not go. I never wanted to leave them, I never wanted to abandon them or my parents, but that's what it felt like. I remember everyone yelling and screaming, and Colin telling me to get out the door and into the car. At the same time, my parents were telling me that if I got in the car and drove away, I would not speak to or see any of them again.

I felt confused, lost, and guilty for wanting to live with Colin, but somehow I got in the car, weeping. As they had threatened, communication was cut off and I wasn't allowed to talk to anyone for a while. Thankfully my siblings secretly wrote letters and managed to get someone to post them to me. That continued connection with them was so precious to me as I adjusted to my new life.

❖ ❖ ❖

Living on the farm with no driver's licence and feeling rather restricted, I looked for work. One farmer up the road hired me to do his bookkeeping. He was another God-send, a man I came to look at as a father figure. Once I had brought his books up-to-date, there was less for me to do, so he introduced me to other farmers in the area who also needed help with bookkeeping. It worked out well, as the farmers didn't need a full-time bookkeeper, so a few hours a week for each of them suited them and me. I ended up working six days a week.

During this time, things with Colin went from difficult to impossible. Most nights Colin went out drinking in town or at the local club. As I was never a big drinker or partygoer, I stayed home on the farm alone most nights. Our relationship was falling apart, and we argued a lot. Most days Colin would yell at me, telling me I was boring and messed up in the head—only not as politely as I have written it!

The situation continued to get worse between us, to the point where we did not have a nice thing to say to each other. During one argument, Colin told me that I was messed up and that I should see a psychiatrist. Well, one of the farmers' wives I worked for was a psychiatrist, so I asked her if I could see her. I broke down, then poured out my life and hurt to her over the space of a few months. During this time, even though the psychiatrist was not talking to me about God, I realised that I had stopped pressing into God and began to see how much more I needed Him.

Meanwhile, Colin went out drinking almost every night, and one of my female friends, who went out in the same group told me that he had been flirting with her and even tried to kiss her. My heart broke. I was still not talking to my family and was not sure what I was going to do. I had lost my trust in Colin. Compounding things was the fact that an ex-girlfriend had moved to the area as a teacher, and Colin would flirt with her in front of me. I tried to ignore it at first, but later tried to bring it up in a discussion, which went very badly.

Around this time, I fell pregnant. When I found out, I was so scared. Colin had always said that if I fell pregnant, he would send me back to the city. From the start of our relationship, he had been very clear that he never wanted children. My fears were amplified by the fact that we were not very close. In fact, at that stage, I believed that being sexually intimate with him was the only way I was keeping him with me and preventing him from cheating on me. Still, I worked the courage up to tell him I was pregnant. I was gaining weight and knew I couldn't keep quiet for much longer. This led to a huge argument. Sadly, a few days later, I had a miscarriage while

I was at work. Colin wasn't there at the time, and for many years believed I was lying.

From that point on, the distance between us grew. I was still hearing about Colin flirting and visiting the female teachers at the local school. He seemed to be focused only on himself, leaving me once again to be the responsible one who made sure everything else was taken care of. In the midst of all of this, the farmer Colin was working for advised him that he had to find another job as he could not afford a manager any longer. Fortunately, he was able to find another job in the same area with wonderful people.

◆ ◆ ◆

It wasn't just our relationship that was complicated; so were our extended family relationships. Colin's parents still did not accept me, and whenever they visited, I had to go away for the weekend, which hurt me terribly. Eventually I met with them, and we agreed to work on our relationship and to get to know one another properly.

My own family was dispersed all over the place and it was hard to keep in touch with them. At one point I woke up to find my folks sleeping outside our locked gate in their vehicle because they had nowhere to live. They stayed with us for a while and I always did my best to send money. I would often buy food and supplies, or help in any way we could.

The move to the new farm meant that my two younger siblings who I had been able to maintain contact with began visiting more often and staying with us for holidays. Over time my other siblings and I regained contact, and they began spending weekends with us. Having family around me again took my focus off my broken relationship. Then, I got news that Mom had cervical cancer. I decided to help her, and she came and stayed with me for a little while until she had worked things out and was due to have her operation.

As time continued, more of my family who I had not had contact with for some time began to visit. Around this time, I started to see Dad again, which was exceedingly difficult because he continued to bring up the past, especially after a few drinks. I never wanted to pursue my relationship with him, but Colin insisted I try, so I did. Soon, my family members became Colin's drinking buddies, and again I began taking on responsibilities for everyone I could. This helped keep my focus off Colin and me, and ensured all my feelings stayed inside.

One weekend Colin's family planned a trip to Kariba for the 'Tiger Tournament'. I was out of the room when they were speaking about it, but as we were driving home that night Colin advised me that he was going fishing the following weekend. His family, who he had not seen in a while, were coming with friends from South Africa and they would all be going together. I was not invited.

I went quiet, which I had become good at doing. Isolation and the silent treatment were my go-to coping mechanisms. On the hour-long drive home, all I did was stare out my window. I didn't want him to see the tears running down my cheeks.

The week ahead was tense, and I looked forward to going to work every day. It was a chance to escape what was happening at home and get my mind on other things. But talking to my friends at work about the situation didn't really help—it only made me feel more hurt, and angrier towards Colin. At the end of the week when I got home from work, Colin wanted me to give him money to buy some things to go fishing with, but I said no. Yet another argument ensued. I thought I better talk to him. Deep down I was hoping he would not go fishing if I spoke nicely to him. I wanted him to be sorry for making the decision without me and to show he was putting me and my feelings first. But the main reason I wanted him to stay home was my fear that while he was away, he would get drunk, find another woman, and then leave me.

That night when I tried to talk to him, Colin yelled at me and walked away. I don't know why, but for some reason people walking away from me has always made my blood boil. I got so angry I took his plate, which had his dinner on it, and threw it onto the floor. Colin looked at me, asked me if he was supposed to be scared, then laughed and walked further away. Well, for the first time in my life, I experienced anger to the point where I felt numb, like I did not care what happened next.

I picked up a steak knife and followed Colin into the dining room, where I grabbed him and held the knife close to his neck and challenged him to push me further, to make me angry. I don't remember all I said, but I knew I was waiting for him to fight back. It was only seeing the shock in his eyes which made me back away. I decided that I needed to go for a drive to calm down.

I am not proud of this moment in my life and wish I had never got to the point I did that night. In the moment, I felt strong and in control, but that was so far from the truth. All I had done was push Colin and me further apart and open up a side of me that terrified me. He packed up and set off on his fishing trip. I was convinced he would come back with a new woman and dump me.

The week he was away, I had a lot of time to think. I began to seek God and ask for forgiveness. As I pressed into God that week, I got a revelation that no matter what I did I could not command, force, or convince Colin to love me, or prevent him from cheating on or leaving me. I wept so much that week as I took steps of surrender and letting Colin go. I kept hearing the saying, "If you love something enough, let it go; if it was meant to be yours, it will come back."

This wasn't really what I wanted to do, to be honest. I wanted to get Colin to see me as worthy and to treat me accordingly. I wanted him to make me feel better about myself, which was obviously not happening. That week, I was able to come to a place where I was willing to accept whatever choice Colin made when he returned from his trip.

Colin did come home to me—thankfully, with no other woman in his life. A year and a half later he even proposed to me and I accepted. But nothing had changed in our relationship. We simply carried on in our brokenness.

STEP OUT OF THE WILDERNESS

Are there any relationships where you are trying to control the responses and choices of the other? Ask the Holy Spirit to reveal what fears are driving your need for control. Invite Him to minister the perfect love of the Father to your heart and to empower you to surrender that relationship to His care.

CHAPTER FIVE

Do not remember the former things, nor consider the things of old. Behold, I will do a new thing, now it shall spring forth; Shall you not know it? I will even make a road in the wilderness and rivers in the desert.

Isaiah 43 v 18-19

Colin's proposal was not anything close to romantic. We had bought a ring together which had sat in the cupboard for a few weeks. When he finally got around to asking me to marry him, we agreed on a long engagement—more than four years, in fact! But early the following year, I was sure I was pregnant again. I was too scared to tell Colin, but decided to buy a pregnancy test while I was in town for a meeting with my boss. Before we left town, I popped in to see Colin's mom. By this time. we had become close, which felt somewhat magical to me given our history.

When I told Colin's mom that I thought I was pregnant and had bought a pregnancy test, she was so excited, but I made her give me her word she would not say anything and said I would let her know once I had done the test. Early the next morning I did the test, and it was positive. Still too scared to tell Colin, I left the test on the sink in the bathroom, knowing that when he came home for breakfast he would go to wash his hands first. When he saw it, he called out from the bathroom that it was not true. He didn't believe me and wanted me to see a doctor. I booked an appointment, called Colin's mom to tell her I was going for a blood test, and told nobody else about the pregnancy.

The day I was to get the blood results back, I went into town to pick up some of my family who were coming to stay with us for the weekend, and on the way back I stopped for my appointment. My family came and sat in the waiting room with me. To my horror, the doctor came out, looked at me and said, "Congratulations, you are pregnant," and walked away. My family, as well as everyone else in the waiting room, stared at me. I wanted the ground to eat me up. We got home, and before I could tell Colin the results, my family were congratulating him and telling him how the doctor had told everyone. Colin was not impressed at all.

That night I called his mom and whispered over the phone to her that it was confirmed. I told her to visit the following weekend so we could tell them, but asked her to keep the news to herself until then. When Colin's parents came and we told them about the baby, they were determined that we should get married immediately. In their minds, there was no other option. I didn't wanted to get married and nor did Colin, not yet—and we told them so!

Colin's mom had been diagnosed with breast cancer a few years before, had a mastectomy, and had been in remission for nearly a year at this point in time. Now she started telling us we needed to get married as the cancer was back and she didn't know how long she would be around. It was important to her to see her only son get married. The pressure was now on! I had a feeling deep down that it was not right, but we gave in to them, and when I was five months pregnant, we got married. One month before the baby was due, Colin's mom passed away. I struggled with her passing, as she had become both my best friend and mom. I didn't know what to do. I was so scared of being a bad mother and failing my baby; without my mom-in-law I didn't know how I would cope.

Nothing about my pregnancy was easy. I was ill throughout and huge like an elephant—the skin on my stomach was thinning so much I was sure if you shone a torch on my tummy, you would see through it. Our daughter Nicole was two weeks overdue, and after sixty-two hours of labour, I was eventually induced. However, the gynaecologist was due to fly out on holiday, even with the induction my labour was progressing too slowly, and the umbilical cord was around Nicole's neck, so it was decided to do a caesarean. I had general anaesthetic, which by now, I was very happy about as I had no pain relief up to this point. Nicole was a large baby, so I doubt I would have managed natural birth at all. But she was beautiful and healthy, and from the moment I saw her, my heart and life changed forever. She even melted Colin's heart. The hospital security had to force him out of the hospital at midnight—funny, when you think he never wanted children!

As a new mom, I couldn't keep doing all the bookkeeping for the different farmers six days a week, so I took up a full-time job in a tannery where I was very blessed to be able to take Nicole to work with me. I started as the administration manager and then progressed to the position of manager, working with fantastic people, some of whom became very good friends of mine. I loved my job. But then, not too long after having Nicole, I fell pregnant again.

Colin and I had agreed that we wanted to have our children close together, but this was another difficult pregnancy and again I was sick throughout. Due to the first caesarean and the second baby being so close, and seeing the baby was not yet in position to be born, the gynaecologist scheduled another caesarean. The date was set, but when the day came, I felt something was wrong. It was a public holiday in Zimbabwe, which meant the best doctors were not available, and we got whoever was rostered on. The only doctor I knew and was confident with, was the gynaecologist. The other problem was that because of my long recovery after Nicole's birth, I had asked for an epidural rather than general anaesthetic, but the anaesthetist arrived late which meant I had to have a spinal block instead. All my concerns were becoming a reality!

I was taken into theatre and had the spinal, but it didn't work. It was injected into my spine wrongly, so I felt every cut the surgeon made. I was already feeling confused and scared. When the midwife climbed on the theatre table to push my baby down, it was yet another thing I was not expecting nor had been explained to me. By the time they got the baby out, I was sure that all my internal organs were on the floor. The pain I experienced that day I will never forget.

At that point, I received even more concerning news—the doctors had miscalculated my dates and our son was, in fact, seven weeks premature. They put my little boy on my chest, but he was not breathing and was blue. This scared me. We had already lost our first child and now, with no paediatrician there, our little boy, Nathan, got instant pneumonia and was fighting for his life. We were told he had a fifty percent chance of survival at the best. I could not move—due to the spinal anaesthetic, a lot of the fluid around my brain had seeped out down my spine. My head felt so heavy that I literally could not lift it off the bed. I was that way for a few days and couldn't see Nathan, which was so hard. Colin never told me how bad Nathan really was because he knew I was stressed already.

The day I did get to see my baby, I could not stop crying; he had pipes and things everywhere. I wasn't allowed to touch him as he was in an incubator with oxygen to help him breathe. I felt torn because I wanted to be home with Nicole, and I also wanted to be with Nathan. Nathan fought a good fight and came out on top, thank the Lord. We had a few hard times with Nathan being seven weeks premature, but thankfully he was a big baby, weighing over three kilograms at birth, which gave him an advantage. Still, he had to be watched for a few years as he easily got colds which went to his chest, and he got a lot of ear infections too.

◆ ◆ ◆

After some time, Colin's boss gave us the option to purchase a farm from him, which we agreed to. We were very excited that this would be our future farm. But in 1998, the government in Zimbabwe began taking farmland away from white farmers for political reasons. We, along with many other white farmers, were affected by this. One morning in 2000, around 1 a.m. we woke to the sound of big trucks with people shouting and drums being hit. We felt ill, knowing they were there to take the farms. At first the farm invaders, who were referred to as war veterans, dwelt on the farm with us. Colin learnt to negotiate to keep them happy and peaceful. But even so, we had many days where Colin's, mine, or other people's lives on the farm were threatened with guns, sickles, machetes, or other things. It was very stressful, to say the least, and extremely scary.

Then one morning in 2002 we got up and discovered the invaders didn't want to talk anymore. They surrounded our home, separating Colin and me, the other manager, and Colin's boss' relatives from one another. They were shouting and screaming at us, telling us that we were white pigs who needed to go back to England, even though we were never from there. The invaders surrounded our home and held us under house arrest for five days. They did this to the boss' relatives and the other manager too. The other manager was a black man, who they threatened to kill because he had chosen to work for a white farmer. That day, Colin stood in between the manager and the invaders and negotiated to save his life, and for his family and him to leave the farm safely.

Colin had to negotiate many times in those five days to protect everyone, including his work force. We were pushed around, threatened, and spat at amongst other things. To be honest, with all we were being subjected to, we really thought we were not going to survive. We watched staff members being brutally beaten, some having almost every bone broken; others were beaten and then had fuel poured over them to be burnt alive. The invaders would throw things through our house windows, demanding food and drink. They told us all the things they would do to us if we did not obey them. That was scary, more than scary! We knew they were capable of doing anything and would not care. It was the longest five days of our lives. When they let us go, we left that farm and did not look back. We packed all we could and left. Everything we left behind that day, the invaders claimed as theirs. Many farmers lost their lives; we were among the lucky ones. Property and material items had no value to us at that point. When you are that close to being tortured and losing your life, you start to realise what is truly valuable!

We moved up the road near the tannery I was managing, but the invaders from the farm followed us there and would sit outside the gates to intimidate us. For a while, Colin found a few jobs here and there helping other farmers negotiate and get their assets and families off the farms. During this time, invaders came to the tannery and held us hostage, claiming the tannery as theirs too. It was scary, as Nicole and Nathan came to work with me, and I knew the invaders were capable of anything. The worst thing was that we had no police support at all; in fact some of the invaders claiming the land and businesses were in high powered positions and therefore unstoppable.

Eventually Colin found a farm manager job closer to the capital city, where we decided it best that I stay home for a little while with the children. With the farm manager position we had to live on the farm, but the house was not ready for us, so we rented a cottage in the meantime. Being home alone with no other interaction made most days feel long and lonely. When we had the children, I was hoping Colin would be different and that things would get better, but that was not the case. Things got harder and I grew cold towards Colin.

◆ ◆ ◆

One day we met the cottage owner's son, and in that moment, something changed in me. When the young man came over and introduced himself, my heart raced. He turned to leave, and I found myself commenting on his looks, loud enough that Colin heard, though hopefully not the young man. Suddenly, I felt that my heart had been stolen. I couldn't explain why, but knew that was what happened. This young man was good-looking and a gentleman. Some days while I was outside playing with the kids and he was passing by, he would say hi and check on us. Every time he did that, he took more and more of my heart.

I prayed to God and asked Him to forgive me for my feelings towards this man. I felt like an adulteress all over again. One day I confessed to one of my sisters how I felt about him, but otherwise, I worked hard to keep my feelings hidden and never told the man how I felt. I knew it was wrong. As I wrestled with all my conflicting emotions, I kept telling myself my feelings were driven by the distance between Colin and I; that my feelings were not real. I found myself back in a fantasy world in my head.

I always prayed that Colin would be saved, but it got to a point when

I just decided that I couldn't carry on this way any longer. I decided I didn't want the kids growing up in the environment they were in, as we were not a happy, united family. I told God I couldn't do it anymore, that I tried and had nothing left. I then told Colin that it was not working, just like I had told him over previous years, only this time I wanted a divorce. Colin thought I was joking when I mentioned this, and told me that I was nothing without him and I needed to remember that. This only made me more sure that leaving was the right thing.

At this stage we had moved out of the cottage and onto the farm Colin managed, and I didn't see much of the man I had feelings for, although we had all become friends and would catch up from time to time. The weekend after I told Colin I wanted a divorce, Mom came to visit and I shared where I was at with her. That night, unknown to me, Mom spoke to Colin and told him that she was concerned because she felt I was very serious about leaving.

After Mom spoke to Colin, he asked to talk with me, so when the kids were in bed, we went for a drive. I told him that I had fallen for another man. I told him honestly who it was, and that the man was unaware of my feelings as I had said nothing and I believed the man never saw me as anything other than a friend. I explained it had become harder for me to ignore my attraction to him, and how I realised just how much we had in common and how easily we laughed and joked—something Colin and I didn't have. After we talked, Colin asked me to give him another chance, which I was very reluctant to do, to say the least. I told him I would think about it.

When I went to bed that night, I prayed and asked God to show me what to do, and as I lay there, I heard in my spirit, "I gave you a second chance!" That was all I needed to hear to know. I wasn't going to leave.

A few nights later, I told Colin I would give him another chance, but we needed counselling and if he messed up after that chance, it was over. He agreed, and I booked us into a twelve-week marriage course which was run at a Christian counselling center. Colin was not a Christian; in fact, he often mocked me for my beliefs and for praying. He let me know he was not planning on becoming a Christian either. To his credit, he saw the course out, and he tried hard and was different for a while, but after the course had finished, he quickly slipped back into his old ways.

I enrolled in other counselling courses, including one called 'Boundaries'. The content built me up and gave me confidence; it also gave me new insights into myself and helped me realise that my attraction to this man was in part because the way he talked to me and treated me made me see myself as deserving of love. He made me feel worthy. The courses helped me start to really know and understand myself.

During this time, I began a new job working for a Christian couple, Joh and Tracey. At home, we had a few instances with bad spirits in the house. In Africa, witchcraft is a very real thing and the spiritual realm is a very real realm. As we were having these issues at home, I spoke to Joh and asked if he would be able to come pray through our home with me. He agreed and brought a friend with him named Theunis. When they came over, they spoke and prayed with us. Colin was hesitant but followed as we went through the house praying and reading aloud the Word of God.

In one of our rooms, Theunis asked if we knew of a death in the room? Colin laughed and told him the cat had died in there. We kept praying, and as we moved into the next room, there was a sound like a gust of wind and something pushed past Colin so fast and hard that it nearly knocked him over. Well, he very quickly started to take the praying seriously. After Joh and Theunis had prayed and were leaving, they said if we needed them again, they would come back.

A few nights later, Colin woke me up early hours of the morning to tell me he had a dream and felt God had shown him that if he didn't turn to God, he would lose me, the kids, and everything, because the devil would destroy it all. Colin decided to give his life to God and ask Jesus into his life. From that point, we were blessed to be discipled by Theunis and his wife, Deidre, who became very good friends of ours.

Colin immediately experienced change! It was early that week he gave his life to God and on the Friday, one of my brothers who was also one of Colin's drinking buddies, came over to visit and after shaking Colin's hand, swung to me and asked what I had done to Colin. Colin then shared he had given his life to God and had accepted Jesus as his Saviour and Lord. Colin used to swear terribly but for some reason, now he would get earache when he swore, so he stopped. His bad drinking habit came to an end; he just stopped desiring the alcohol like he did before. I felt hope rise in my heart and a gratitude to God that is unexplainable. Things began improving between Colin and I, although truthfully, a part of me was waiting for him to go back to his old ways. But instead, Colin continued to change for the better. His love and passion for God began growing, and in turn our relationship slowly began to take a positive turn too.

◆ ◆ ◆

As things improved between Colin and I and our relationship became healthier, I started to unravel things in our history. I began to realise that with Colin, I never really listened to God's leading from the beginning. From the time our friendship turned to feelings that night I touched Colin's hand, my mind took a different direction to the way God was leading my heart. I was blind to that then, and questioned through those difficult years how it was that I ended up in yet another situation where I was broken, lonely, and hurting so badly. But the Holy Spirit began to reveal things to me . . .

You see, Colin was and still is a great guy, but he had faced a lot of difficulties and challenges in his life. He had often felt alone and unwanted; in fact, right from the outset of his mom's pregnancy, abortion had been suggested, but she refused. So, she ended up a single parent who had no idea what to do. She had been raised in a family where she did not feel loved and she too had a tough life. She knew she never wanted her child to feel the way she felt but wasn't sure how she could do better. Colin was never given boundaries from the start, and he gave his mother a hard time. Unable to manage this little boy, she asked her parents to raise him for a while. His grandparents loved him endlessly, and this was the only time Colin had discipline and boundaries in his life. But eventually he ended up back with his mom who got married to a man who formally adopted Colin.

Not long after being back home, Colin was sent off to boarding school. He was only seven years old. Colin only went home for holidays, and even then, not all holidays. In Africa, there are three school terms a year, meaning the terms are long. He was bullied badly at school and had no one to love, protect, lead, guide, or comfort him. Consequently, he became very independent from a young age. All of this caused Colin to close up and shut people out; he didn't know how to love himself or others.

Through God's teachings and guidance, I learnt that each of our histories matter. If we are not taught how to deal with our past, it often leads to negative choices and heavy consequences. I started to see that from the very beginning with Colin, I should have recognised that he struggled with commitment and was only focused on himself. These attributes should not have come as a shock to me because I had seen and heard it all before we dated each other, when he shared so much with me about his life and choices.

I too had no idea what to do, and so I chose to get together with someone who deep down I knew would hurt me, because I felt that I had become a strong person. I thought that I would be fine and that it would all work out, that I could cope with it. I clung to the little love signs I got from Colin along the way instead of seeking God first. And once I had slept with Colin, I felt that in God's eyes, I was now married to him. I believed this—and still do—because God's Word says a man and a woman become one flesh after being joined together; a very deep connection comes from our sexual intimacy.

Me believing I was strong and able to cope with the hurt in the relationship landed me in a lot of heartache, anger, and confusion. It even led to me bringing innocent children into the dysfunctional situation (I would never change having my two amazing children though!). I was only seeing the truth of it all on the other end, because everything had been stripped away. Now I had to look at myself and my choices, not the excuses!

I still struggled with trusting Colin. To be honest, it was so bad I thought I would never trust him again. As we talked and time went on, Colin began to share other things that he had hidden, like struggling with pornography, and although it was not something I wanted to hear at this point, God knew what He was doing. Things had to come out for healing to start; when things are brought out into the open, the devil has no strongholds left. Theunis and Deidre began coming to our house more often to disciple us and teach us more of God's Word. This was a time of a lot of growth and it was good, because Colin and I were learning to open up to one another, and we were growing together. Amazing things began to happen in our little family as we grew, like improvement in our kids' health, and in Colin's relationship with them.

After delving into our histories and understanding how they impacted our relationship, I began to wonder about the kind of life my parents had. *What had caused them to be the way they had been with me?* I decided to start the conversation with my mom and seek to understand what had happened in her life.

◆ ◆ ◆

Mom never shared things with us kids, not that I remember anyway. As she began to share her story, my heart softened and all the anger, pain, hurt, and rejection I had felt towards and for Mom, began to dissipate. I realised, as she shared her story, how dysfunctional her family had been. She was from a divorced family with many children and her parents were no longer on talking terms. Like me, Mom had to help look after her family members. And also like me, she never had her parents' love or approval. There were many nasty things said to and about her through her life. She stayed in an orphanage for a time, and at times, thought she must have been adopted. Mom was also abused in various forms and learnt to become a tough, independent woman. All she longed for was to be important, loved, worthy, and noticed. I realised, as she shared her life experiences with me, that as much as she always wanted children, she had to grow up too fast, with no love and support or direction, and no relationship with God for much of her life. I realised how broken inside Mom was. So much of what she shared of her life painted a picture of my life.

I then began to ask the father figures in my life about their life stories, and discovered they too experienced much brokenness, hurt, hardship, and lack of love and affection. It was no wonder that when the time came for them to parent, they too didn't do it well.

As we grew together, Colin convinced me to reconnect with my dad and get to know him. We often went around to see him and his wife on weekends. Our stays were usually only for the afternoon, and a few times we spent the night but very seldom because I struggled with staying in the house; it reminded me of so much hurt. Once Dad had a few beers, things always got out of hand, just as it did when I was a child, and I decided that as an adult, I would not stay around it. His wife was a nice lady once we got to know each other, but very hard. She never showed any emotion and swore terribly (which I hated), but as I was in their home, I just let it go.

As time went on, all our relationships developed but I still struggled with the guilt I felt for Dad's hurt, something he would remind me of after a few drinks. When I was around Dad, I was always sure to make a stand. I would tell him what I thought and what I didn't like hearing or seeing. As a child I carried it all and as an adult, I didn't want to carry more of it. There were a few times where things got a little heated, and he would throw things, swear at me, and tell me he was disowning me. He frequently threatened to kill himself and made it clear that if he did, it would be my fault and I would have to live with that. Sadly, my children witnessed this and they became scared of him and distanced themselves from him. This was heartbreaking because I remember the love that I saw in Dad's eyes the day he held each of my babies, and his smile as he looked at them. It showed me that behind all the anger, Dad did have a big heart even if it wasn't often seen.

Our visits and getting to understand more about him and his life, really helped me. I realised he wasn't sure how to love us or how to demonstrate that love to us. Not that it is an acceptable excuse, but I had more empathy for him. The more I came to understand my parents, the softer my heart became with them all. I stopped judging them and instead hurt for them. Their own family's choices and later their choices, all had consequences which they were living and experiencing but had never understood. In fact, Dad and Mom both believed God had written it that way to teach them and make them wise. They believed this, as it was what they had been told as children.

As they all shared their life journeys with me over time, I realised how our history, choices of the past, both of ours and of others, have the power to change and impact another life in deep and long-term ways and to affect their future choices—either positively or negatively.

Without God in our lives, *how would we know the right way?* My children have often asked me, "Mom, how is it that you had such a hard life and yet you are such a great mom to us?" It touched my heart to know I had been better for them, and that they could see it. My answer is, "I could only have done what I have done because the Holy Spirit led me each and every step of the way and continues to lead me." I believe God wants to be a part of everything, to be part of all of us, and the Word tells us that too. God will make a way for us as we follow and obey His leading—even when we have to live with tough consequences.

Consequences are the result of something that happens; if you lose your footing, you are going to trip or fall. You cannot escape consequences. We can try to avoid them or reason our way out of them, but it won't work forever. In the end, we will face the consequences. Sometimes those consequences are not due to our doing—they're simply part of living in a fallen world—but as long as we seek God, are obedient and willing, He will get us through. I see trials as consequences; some are easier to understand or explain and others are not so easy. Consequences make facing and dealing with situations a little harder or trickier for us humans. I say this because we use logic and try to make sense of it all and often feel fearful.

It is most certainly not easy; please don't think I am saying it is. Trust me, as I went through my wilderness walk it was hard, it hurt, and I was scared. At times I thought it would be best if I left it all alone and pretended it never happened or existed. But God says that the truth will set us free, and I can testify to that. Believing in God, being obedient, following and loving God, does not mean that things will just go away, that we won't have to face consequences, or we won't be caught up in a wrong choice in the future. But God says He will guide and strengthen us in times of trouble.

God knew that living in this fallen world, we would face many situations and consequences throughout our lives. In His Word, He constantly reassures us that He will be with us and strengthen us as we take our steps in this journey we call *life*.

◆ ◆ ◆

After getting to know my parents more, I felt I needed to get some answers from other people. I decided the next person I approached would be my first abuser. I don't know why I chose them first, but I did, and it was a big mistake. The answers I got made me feel even worse than before—more worthless and less loved. The sting of the abuse felt deeper and more intense. I felt confused. *Why did God stir me to face these things, yet when I tried, my hurt was worse?*

I realised that I had only followed the Holy Spirit's leading to the point of facing my past. Instead of going back to God when I felt he was stirring me to take the next step, I thought, *Well, He must mean I should go and talk to all the people who had been part of my life.* I had missed the point that I was supposed to continually go back to God for direction. I needed to stop thinking that God would only give the starting point and then leave me to figure the rest out. This was all part of the "God doesn't like lazy people" thinking that had been ingrained in me all my life and needed to be dismantled. The truth is that God alone knew exactly what to bring up, and when, and how. When I followed His leading, situations were resolved, hurts healed, trust mended, and love rekindled.

STEP OUT OF THE WILDERNESS

Who or what in your own story is God inviting you to view with new understanding? How does this new understanding reshape your perspective of the past? What step is God inviting you to take in light of this insight?

CHAPTER SIX

And we know that all things work together for good to those who love God, to those who are the called according to His purpose.
Romans 8 v 28

Life in Zimbabwe became increasingly hard and expensive. People were earning millions of Zimbabwe 'dollars', but the value of the currency meant this was equivalent to just a few hundred US dollars. Due to high inflation, everything, even basic commodities, was priced at 'millions' of dollars. We often tried to convert our salaries to US currency so that when the exchange rate improved, we could convert it back to the local currency to gain a few dollars.

At times, when people we knew were crossing the borders into South Africa, Mozambique, or Zambia, we would get them to buy things we needed using our American dollars. This was the only way we could get basic necessities like rice, or sugar and flour, and it was a costly exercise, but with so little food on the store shelves we had no choice. After almost all the farms had been seized there were no exports and no foreign investment into the country, which meant limited availability of food and other basic items. The stress of everyday living alongside personal hardships often felt impossible.

As things in the country became more difficult, a relative of Colin's found a job opportunity for Colin in Sudan, which Colin took. His relative also found a job there for my stepdad at the same time. Colin worked in Sudan for almost two years. Sudan is in the northern part of Africa, while

Zimbabwe is the most southern part of the continent. Knowing we would be apart for some time, I began the task of looking for accommodation in Harare so I could be settled in a house with the children before Colin left.

I was sure Mom would go and live with one of my sisters after my stepdad went to Sudan, but as conversations went on, the suggestion of Mom living with me and the kids came up. I was not happy with the idea, as we had only just started to build our relationship, and at that point, things were still very tense between us. I was also concerned about the extra financial cost. I prayed on it, sure that God wasn't stirring me to have my mom stay with us, but as I prayed God gave me peace about the decision, so Mom and I moved into the house together.

From the outset, I decided that it was best if everything was agreed on in writing. So, we had all four of our names on the lease. I bought a notebook which came to be known as 'the black book', where all costs, no matter what they were, were recorded, along with who had paid, how the cost was to be split, and who owed what. I did this to ensure that everything was kept fair and in the open. I often got mocked by other family members for doing this, but it worked. It kept the peace, and no one could say anything false. Soon after moving into the house, the two men left for Sudan.

Mom came to work with me every day and helped me, as she struggled to find a job. This was good in the sense that it enabled us to get to know each other more, but it was difficult being around each other twenty-four hours a day. I was the General Manager of the business and with school hours being from 7.30 a.m. to 1 p.m., I had the kids with me in the afternoons.

The child minder came to work with me when the children were there, but with Colin going away, I decided to request that we employ someone to take over my role. I would then work alongside the incoming General Manager, running the finances.

We found a wonderful man named Malcolm, who did a great job when he started, but not long after he began, he got sick from what we thought were stomach ulcers. He collapsed and was rushed to the hospital where he was operated on and diagnosed with advanced cancer of the stomach.

◆ ◆ ◆

Malcolm was funny, secure, and had happy characteristics that drew people to him. When Malcolm began working with me, he asked Mom and me about our beliefs. Mom had turned back to God by now, so we shared our faith with him, but he said he never believed. After his diagnosis, he opened up and told us his life story.

He had two daughters but no one else. I felt stirred to visit him daily after his operation, and to take him what he needed, as he had become bedridden. Soon, his daughters arrived to be with him. One evening when we were visiting, I felt the Holy Spirit prompt me to talk to Malcolm about God. I shared how God loved him, but could see he was getting sleepy, so I said I would come back to see him the next day. As I was about to stand up, I asked him if I could pray aloud for him. Every other day I had prayed silently while I sat with Malcolm, but this day he slid his hand into mine and softly said, "Yes, please." His daughters went outside with Mom to talk to her, and holding his hand, I prayed for him. As I said "Amen," he looked at me with bright, wide eyes and said, "Neena, I want to know the God you know, and I want to have Him in my life."

I will never forget those words or that evening. With my eyes full of tears and my heart overflowing, I prayed with Malcolm as he gave his life to God and invited Jesus into his life. We prayed for the Holy Spirit to fill him, and as we were ending the prayer, I saw a vision so clearly that this friend of mine was going to heaven. In the moment, Malcolm's eyes opened wide. He smiled from ear to ear and said, "Neena, I know I am going to heaven. I feel God with me."

I said goodnight and walked out of the room crying. As we made our way to the car, Mom asked me what was wrong. I told her Malcolm gave his life to God. That night I woke up with a fright. In that moment, as I opened my eyes, I saw Malcolm in front of me, and I knew he had gone. Mom woke too, running into the room to tell me she had seen him, and she knew he had gone. Within seconds my phone rang. It was his daughters; they were crying and telling me he had gone, but said that he was smiling and looked peaceful in a way they had never seen before.

◆ ◆ ◆

After a few months of sharing a house and doing life together, Mom and I had a huge argument. It had been building for a long time. Mom would say or do things that bothered me and I would just be quiet, but I never really let go of it all. Instead, I stored it with all the other hurts and things I had not yet faced or dealt with. I can't even remember how the argument began, but it was a big one. Mom told me she would move out, to which I replied that she could go if she wanted. I was yelling at her, telling her she had no right to give me advice on what to do or how to do it, as she had done nothing for me in my life. I told her that she had never been there for me, so what made her think she could now? I can still see her face, even as I type this—the shock, hurt, and shame written all over her face as her eyes filled with tears. I turned around and walked to my bedroom. I was so angry!

In my room, I sat and argued with God, asking Him what kind of sense of humour He had to get us to live together? As I sat there, I felt led to write Mom a letter. God provided the words. It was a short note, and the only part I remember was the part where I said I forgave her for everything and that I was handing motherhood back to her. I never fully understood the motherhood part when I wrote it. I walked to her bedroom where she was lying on her bed, gave her the note, and walked out. I went to the loungeroom, and when I got there the telephone rang. I gathered myself and answered it. It was one of my sisters. She was crying on the phone. I asked her what was wrong, and she said she would be okay but asked to talk to mom. That surprised me as I was always the one members of my family would ask for, or ask help from, but I said okay and called out to Mom.

Mom came, and I watched her as she sat there with the phone to her ear. I heard her ask if she could call my sister back, then she got up and walked away. Within minutes the phone rang again. This time it was one of my brothers. He sounded worried and panicked, so I asked if he was okay and what was wrong. He said he had a problem, but could he talk to our mom? I was now very unsure of what was happening, but I called Mom and once again she came to the phone. She silently listened, then repeated her previous sentence, asking to call back later. She hung the phone up, saying nothing to me. Still angry, I was not going to ask her what was happening. I got up and walked to my bedroom. I sat down on my bed wrestling with my emotions and curiosity about the two calls, when Mom walked in and yelled at me to take the letter back. On it, she had written, "Sure, Bud," a saying we would use if we didn't believe someone or something. I felt the Holy Spirit stir me in that moment not to touch that note ever again. I raised my hands up and said, "No Mom, I will never take it back." Mom looked at me and said she was going to post it on the community noticeboard then, and she walked away.

I was trying to make sense of it all when Mom came back in and told me what the two calls were about. She told me that for so long, everyone including her and my other parents, looked to me for help and direction, and since I handed her the letter, the phone calls were for her, asking for her help and direction. Mom said she felt she didn't know what to say or do, and that I had taken over as mother in the family many years ago. This was something I never knew she saw or felt, or that deep down it hurt her. I was amazed, and realised that in that moment of being obedient to God, He did what His Word said and restored what had been destroyed. He had put things back into their rightful place, with Mom as the mother of the family. That was why He led me to write about handing back motherhood!

From that night on, everyone kept coming to, talking to, or calling for Mom, and our relationship took a new turn: For the first time I could truly say that I loved her. We began to have long, deep conversations very openly about my childhood and past, and her past, and why she did things she did. God amazed me as He led Mom and opened up her heart and her ears to hear. She never got angry like she used to; instead, after we had chatted, sometimes hours, minutes or even days later, Mom would apologise for the things we had discussed, and I too would apologise for the things I did that were wrong and hurtful. Not only did God renew my love for her, but also my respect grew. I got to know her, and we built a relationship. This happened over a period of six months. Then, what amazed me more, was that Mom began approaching each of her children and talking to them about the past, attempting to work with them to build their relationships. I even grew to admire her for this.

It was a privilege watching God restore Mom and her relationship with each of us. You see, I learnt that only God can touch each of us that deeply, and that His revelations are truly life-changing. I began to realise that God knew when each of us would be in the right place or have the mindset to be willing to hear. If Mom and I had moved into a home together when I was first questioning God about the way Mom had been to me, I would never have seen the healing, restoration and building I witnessed, because neither of us would have been willing or ready, and it would have resulted in more hurt. Does God have the perfect timing? I believe it with all I am.

◆ ◆ ◆

I also had to learn to trust God's timing with Colin so far away. The decision for Colin to go to Sudan had been soaked in prayer. We knew it was going to be hard on our family being separated for long lengths of time and were concerned about the children growing distant from their father. We wanted to be confident it was the right decision so when the offer first presented itself, and again as the time drew near for him to leave, we prayed. We sensed God confirming it was the right thing to go. However, we would need to lean on this confidence in the days to come.

With Colin away I quickly learnt what being a single parent was all about, and the stress it brings. I never wanted the kids to grow apart from Colin, so I tried to arrange video calls every night we possibly could so the kids could see him and chat. But after only a few weeks of Colin being gone, the kids stopped asking for him. They never wanted to chat or see him on those calls. They were so little, my heart hurt for them.

I had a new routine now which did not include Colin. I made decisions every day without him. With each day and each decision, it became normal for me to do it alone, even though at night when I lay in bed, I felt the weight of it on my shoulders. I would cry myself to sleep clinging to a shirt or jacket of Colin's just to somehow feel he was still close to me, to smell his scent again.

Daily living in a country where inflation changed every hour or less was incredibly stressful to navigate alone. The basic necessities cost a lot extra and had to be negotiated, and the exorbitant prices meant constant planning just to survive. It was normal to have no electricity or running water in our home for up to a week, sometimes longer. Most times when the water came in, it was very late at night or in the early hours of the morning, and we would jump out of bed to fill every bucket and pot, as well as the sink and bath, and top up the swimming pool, to get us through until the next time it came back. For electricity we used a generator.

We had to be careful to never drive home the same way two nights in a row because we were constantly being watched or followed. Fuel was often in short supply, and we'd have to queue at a service station for days, waiting for it to arrive, unable to leave the car because it would be stolen or have parts stripped off it. Other times we would try to source fuel on the black market. It was a full-time job trying to make sure everything was covered and all the bills were paid. And then there were all the people to look after.

Every day I would check on or call certain family members including Dad to make sure they had what they needed and were all safe and healthy. But the hardest thing was raising the kids alone, and especially looking after them when they were sick. With little to no sleep I would still have to get up and work the next day. I constantly felt unsafe even though we had bars on the windows, a barred door on the other side of a normal door, and six-foot-high walls with razor wire above them and an electric gate surrounding our house. All of this was meant to help us feel safe in our home, but the threats just never stopped, never.

I was frequently abused verbally by locals at supermarkets for being white and told to go back to England because "that's where white people should be." Work had stresses of its own. With no money in the country and no cash at the banks, customers couldn't pay for products, which made it difficult to pay staff. Often the management would not get paid in full or on time as there was only enough to pay the other staff, further compounding the struggle of everyday life. When we could pay staff, getting money from the bank was so hard that we would have to go to the larger local supermarkets and make agreements to buy cash from them. This would include an administration fee for the agreement which was very costly. 'Constant stress' was how life was explained in Zimbabwe. Yet Colin, on the other hand, seemingly had everything. He had water, electricity, food as and when he needed it, he was comfortable, and even though it was a war-torn country he said he felt safe, something I absolutely did not feel.

It was seven long months before he was able to come home for a visit. His leave was for eight days, two of which were lost in travel time. The remaining days were not enough for the kids to get used to him. They were hesitant around him. If he said anything to them, they would look back at me and ask me if that was okay, and if I never answered, they would not do what he asked. It ripped my heart out, and I was sure it was doing the same to Colin, although I never asked him. The week flew by, and before we knew it we were back at the airport saying goodbye. When he hugged me, we both began to cry; this time was even harder than the first goodbye all those months before. I had loved the feel of his arms around me again, and with his next visit six months away at least, the enormity of being alone once more was overwhelming. It took me three days to re-gather myself.

◆ ◆ ◆

I soon got back into my routine, and it became more and more normal to deal with life on my own—still as hard as ever, but 'hard' was normal in Zimbabwe. Our chats with Colin at night got shorter, and further apart. I started to worry, feeling like something was going on. It was a feeling that would not go away and grew in intensity with each passing day.

One day, two men come into my office with a gun and asked me for all the money I had on site. We'd just received payment for a huge order which had unfortunately been cancelled. I was expecting the customer back to collect his money, when these guys arrived. Somehow, I was sure they knew of the money I had; it was in the millions. The currency was so devalued then that we were dealing in millions, billions and heading towards trillions. There were numerous people with me in the office including my kids that day, and I didn't want anyone to get hurt, or worse, so I handed the money over. Thankfully, when the customer arrived to collect their money, they understood the situation and were willing to come back the next day, but it fell on me to somehow find the money to be able to reimburse them.

I had set aside some money for the kids' school fees, but it wasn't enough, so I called Colin to see if I could use some of his salary to cover the balance of the money needed. I had to leave numerous messages as I couldn't get hold of him. When he finally called back, he agreed to help but was not happy with the situation. He called a friend, who very quickly organised the money for me. But life only continued to fall apart from there.

One of the areas we were most impacted by was our children's health. Nathan had recurring serious ear infections which meant many trips to emergency centers, while Nicole kept getting a 'sore heart' as she explained it. She had to be raced to the doctors after crying in pain during a school athletics race, and after many visits to a specialist, we discovered that one of the ventricles would stay open too long, causing her heart to be painful and palpitate. In addition to that, she had a heart murmur, though we were told she would grow out of this in time.

That would have all been enough to deal with, but then our home got broken into. Mom and I usually didn't go to sleep until 1-1.30 a.m. to ensure our safety, but at 1.45 a.m. one morning, four men crowbarred the back door of our house off its hinges. We managed to disturb the intruders before they could cut all the padlocks and get in, but it was a long night as we tried to fix the doors.

I called one of my brothers to come help, and on his way, the police stopped him and held my brother for two hours, asking where he was going. He explained and asked the police to join him, but they refused to because I had not shot or injured the intruders. So yet again, there was no police protection for us. When my brother finally turned onto our street, he saw the four men sitting on the outside of my six-foot wall. They had cut the razor wire above the wall to get furniture over the wall. They were waiting for us to go back to sleep before coming back for another attempt! My brother watched quietly as they stood up and started to walk slowly away from the house. Then they suddenly ran away and jumped over the neighbours' wall when my brother honked the horn.

This wasn't the end of things going wrong. Only a few weeks later, when we were travelling home after checking on some of my relatives, two vehicles followed us to our gate. We had an electric gate but as we never had electricity, Mom would go through the little side gate, unlock the padlock, and push the gate open. This time, while she went through the side gate, two vehicles parked behind me to pin me in. I shouted to Mom to be careful, because now I wasn't sure if there were people on the other side of the gate or if she was in danger. Mom ran back out, and I put the vehicle in reverse. I told my kids' child minder to lay on top of the kids to shield them, as I was going to reverse into the vehicles to get us out of the situation. Mom was screaming as she ran towards the one vehicle which was being driven by a woman. The woman must have got a fright because she quickly pulled off, and then the other vehicle followed her. Mom and I watched to see if they were coming back—they did drive slowly past our house, but then kept going.

On all of these occasions, I tried to call Colin to tell him what was happening, but I could never reach him. I started to worry that he had met someone else in Sudan. I knew we had both adapted to our individual lives as they were now, and worried how our marriage was going to survive. During this time, Colin's leave was also postponed to a later date.

When Colin went to Sudan at the start, it was agreed that he would always take leave at the same time as my stepdad. I never wanted to be in the house with my kids without Colin with other males staying over. After everything I had been through during my childhood years, I no longer trusted males. Although Colin's leave was cancelled, my stepdad's was not, so now he was coming back without Colin. I began to think things couldn't get worse. I shouldn't have thought that, however, because soon after, while I was driving, the steering column in my vehicle broke, and we only narrowly avoided a serious accident! Unable to get hold of anyone to help us, Mom and I had to push the car home, up a few steep hills too!

It was just one thing after another. Whenever things seem to be falling apart, I had learnt to start evaluating what I was doing or not doing that was causing a break in God's protection and guidance over us. I feel I need to find where and how I might be a part of it. By knowing my involvement, I can correct the wrong as best as I can.

◆ ◆ ◆

I began to search to find out what I was doing wrong in this instance, and as I prayed, I began to realise that I had grown cold in my heart towards Colin. I felt insecure and believed that he was doing something in Sudan he shouldn't have been. Even though I had gotten used to living alone and having to face everything by myself, I was angry that when I needed Colin, I could not even reach him on the phone, and that he would not rush to reply or call back. I began to see that our family unit was no longer a unit.

As I looked to God, I began to learn how a family unit works. I made a call to Theunis and Deidre and we began to discuss and study this from God's Word. God began to re-mould me more as He showed me that I had cracks in my life, in my everyday living. This was all the devil needed to get in, all he needed for temptation to creep in and distract me. By acting on the temptation and distraction, I had created cracks in God's protection.

I needed to change my thinking, and honestly, I had known this for a while—even before Colin left for Sudan. Before Colin left we studied the Bible and prayed together every day; we were experiencing God's protection and guidance over our family. Praying about Colin going and getting peace, I somehow had the idea that if God opened the door for him to go, then no matter what, things wouldn't go wrong. Well, that wasn't true. When Colin first left, I read the Word every night and watched Christian television, called God-TV. Then as time went on and things got harder, in my exhaustion, I slowed down on reading the Bible and watched less of

God-TV. I always prayed, but it was mostly before bed, so my prayers were short and not really heartfelt.

After realising this, I began to read the Bible again, along with books by inspirational writers, and began to see and understand how I needed God daily. I needed to be refreshed with the Holy Spirit daily; I needed to choose God daily, it didn't just happen. I realised that things were starting to go weird because I was not wholeheartedly seeking and following God in love and truth. I thought, *Well, if God said yes to Sudan, then everything, I mean everything, will be fine and work out perfect*, but I learnt I needed to take all things to God. I had forgotten that God is a gentleman. He doesn't push His way in, but rather waits for us to share everything with Him and invite Him in.

That lesson came clearly to me when Theunis and Deidre shared a story that gave me a better understanding about sharing everything with God and opening up all things to God . . .

A man was living in a huge double-storey house, and every day there was a knock on the door. The man would answer it, and sure enough, every day at the door was an evil presence—let's say this represents the devil and his temptations. The man would open the door, and in would come the evil presence. At the end of each day the man would feel terrible with the way the day went and all that had gone wrong. One day, someone shared with the man about who God was. He gave his life to God and thought, "That's perfect! There will be no more knocks at the door!"

Well, the very next day, there was a knock, and the man skipped over to the door, opened it, and saw the evil presence again. Things happened, he made choices as before, and things went from bad to worse. Confused, the man prayed and questioned God about why this was happening, as he had given his life to Him. The man felt in his spirit, God's response. He knew God was happy that he had invited Him in, but saw that he had only invited Him into a portion of his house, not into every part. This meant that there was still access for the evil presence and his temptations to take control.

The man was not so happy to hear this explanation, as he thought that simply giving his life to God, accepting and inviting Him in, was enough. He decided that chasing the evil presence and all his temptations out of his house every day was hard work. Deep in the man's heart he really wanted to follow God and His ways, but he found it so hard, so he decided if God lived in his lounge room, which was near the front door, then the evil presence would not come back.

So, the next day the man woke up, prayed, and asked God to please come and live in his lounge room, God's presence filled the room. When the doorbell rang, the man opened the door to find the evil presence there with all the same temptations. Again the man prayed and questioned why this happened, and why God had not chased the evil presence off. God revealed that the man had given God the lounge room, and that was where He was. Thinking about it, the man realised that the evil presence never even tried to enter that area.

The next day, the man gave God the entire bottom floor of the house. Again, God's presence filled the area. The man went off to bed, and rose the next day expecting the best day ever. The doorbell rang, he opened the door, and there stood the evil presence yet again. This time, in he came, going straight upstairs. At the end of the day, still confused with the situation, the man prayed, seeking God, and God revealed the same as before, that God's presence was still in the areas he had given for God to occupy. The man realised that the evil presence went straight upstairs and never tried to get downstairs that day.

Finally, after thinking over it, the man went to God in prayer and said, "God, here are my keys to everything. It is your house, not mine; I abide with you." God's presence now filled the entire home. The next morning when the doorbell rang, the man very wearily opened the door, and there was the evil presence. But this time, the presence of God filled the home. The evil presence looked at the man and very quickly turned away and left.

When this story was shared with me, I realised that I was doing the same thing by thinking that because God was in my heart and I loved Him so much, and that we had prayed about Colin going to Sudan, that everything was going to be perfect. I had only given my lounge, representing only a portion of me. I realised that to stay fully protected, I needed to continually give God full access and authority to every part of my 'house', my daily life. I had to meet with God daily, converse with God daily, and be in His Word daily. This came down to my choice. I saw where I was falling short. Now don't get me wrong—temptations still come; in the story, the devil still knocked on the door. But when the man stood strong with God as he answered the door, the devil had to walk away. I realised that each of us has to do this daily, and in a family unit we need to do it together as well, to build our family up and teach our children how and what to do in their lives too.

As I worked through things with God, I came to realise that I was still angry with my wider family. I was hurt by their choices which had so often left me feeling used, alone, unloved, and unworthy. God began to build on my earlier learning, and I realised why I did everything for everyone: I was only doing things to get love and feel love, to be noticed, worthy and treasured, but mostly, so they couldn't blame me for doing wrong or hurting them. When I asked relatives for help and they didn't (or wouldn't), it really hurt me deeply. I remembered the time when my steering column broke and the family only agreed to help with the repairs if I paid them. As I vented my hurt and anger to God, I realised I felt this way because I had helped them so many times, giving up things—particularly money and time—when they needed it. Now, I was in a situation where I needed their help, and instead of help, I got nothing. I was told I needed to pay because my husband was working out of the country earning foreign currency!

As God began to guide me to examine the reasons I helped them, I realised that much of what I did was with the wrong heart. I began to realise that deep down, I felt that since I had never asked for their help before, when I needed them, they should have been there for me without question. Deep down I had expected that this was what they all should have done. After all, I had always helped them! I felt so horrible. I remember thinking, *God please don't ever show anyone how I felt or thought*. I wanted it to stay just between Him and me. But things hidden are a stronghold for the devil to use to control and tempt us, and it becomes our weakness. I knew this.

I came to realise, through God's Word and the Holy Spirit, that He did everything for me, for each of us, because He loved us first and still loves us—that He did everything for us with no strings attached, never thinking we owed Him anything.

I remember God revealing that for every time I had done things with the wrong motive, it was like throwing pearls before swine; that those things can't be a blessing to others if they come with a weight attached, because others feel the attachment. This made sense; I had always felt that among my relatives, everything had an 'I owe you' debt attached to it. I had to repent of thinking they owed me, and that was not easy. I needed to lose the feeling of being owed, and choose to forgive them for everything. Logic was not helping me at that stage, I can assure you. Logic told me that I deserved their help, and how dare they even think about saying I should pay them?! How dare they forget all the times I was there for them, and how dare they brush it off as nothing, brush *me* off as nothing?! For a while, it felt like a war was raging inside of me.

STEP OUT OF THE WILDERNESS

Invite the Holy Spirit to work with you to search your own heart and reveal if there is any offensive way in you that is causing your life to not align with God's plans and purposes. Confess your sin, thank the Father for His grace and forgiveness through Christ, and ask Him what action you need to take to bring this area of your life back in line with the truth of His Word.

CHAPTER SEVEN

These things I have spoken to you, that in Me you may have peace. In the world you will have tribulation; but be of good cheer, I have overcome the world."
John 16 v 33

The day of my stepdad's arrival home was drawing near and I was dreading it. I questioned God. *Why had Colin's leave been cancelled? Why did my stepdad have to come without him?* I struggled with it all for days before I finally went to Mom and spoke to her about everything. We stayed up all night talking about what my stepdad had done, said, and been to me over my lifetime. Afterwards, I felt better that we had talked and that now Mom knew everything—it wasn't just going over and over in my head.

We picked Kevan up from the airport, and that night I lay in bed praying that God would protect my kids. I felt like I couldn't close my eyes, not even for a second; I lay in bed rocking myself and trying to calm down as I prayed and wept to God, begging for Him to step in.

I had never thought of confronting my stepdad about the ways he had hurt and let me down. But as I lay there, I knew I had to in order to move past the things that had happened. I knew he would get mad—that there would be yelling and screaming, and once again I would likely be blamed for everything. Either that or he would outright deny it all. I felt a deep fear rising within me, slowly taking control of me. As I wrestled with this, I felt God stirring me to write a letter, just as He had stirred me with Mom all those months back. So, I jumped up, not sure what to write or how to word it. I grabbed a notebook and pen, and began to write. I can't remember what I wrote but I knew everything was covered. It was a rather long letter. When I finished, I was unsure about how and when I should give it to him. I lay back down on my bed to think, and for a moment, I closed my eyes.

◆ ◆ ◆

We had the most beautiful Staffordshire Terrier named Shane. She was our first baby. Living in Zimbabwe, we had her sleep inside the house for fear of her being poisoned by thieves. We had trained her that at a certain time at night, we would let her out for a toilet break and that was it until the morning—but she knew that if she really needed to go to the toilet she could jump up on the side of the bed and tap us numerous times with her paws. Well, that night when I closed my eyes, I was woken up by Shane tapping me with her front paws as if to say, "Get up now."

I woke up with a fright, realising I had dozed off. I looked at my doorway, which was directly at the end of the passage and saw the passage was lit up. Panic set in. Shane ran to my doorway and then back to me and jumped up again as if to say, "You really need to get up."

I moved to the doorway, and as I looked up, no lights were on in the passage, but I saw a very large figure in the passageway. I began shaking my head, thinking I must still be sleeping and dreaming. Looking up again, I realised I was seeing an angel, a beautiful, bright angel, who from shoulder to shoulder filled the entire passageway between my parents' door and my children's door. As I was looking at the angel's face, he tipped his head at me and looked like he was smiling. The light that filled the room was so different; it was crisp. I could see no shadows where normally light causes casting of shadows, and I could feel a gentle warmth, like it was filling the passageway, which bought a feeling of peace and calm.

I staggered back to bed trying to figure out what I had just witnessed, wanting to be sure it was not a dream. In that moment, I felt God's presence and, in my spirit, I heard, "I am protecting them for you; you only need to trust Me."

I felt that in being obedient to writing the letter, I allowed God to take control and I believe He woke me up using Shane, so I could witness His answer to my prayer. I fell asleep again for an hour before I had to get up for work, but that hour felt like a full night's sleep. When I got to work and saw Joh arrive, I went to him and asked him if he believed in angels. He smiled and shared how he had come to see an angel, one so big that it stood over his home and he knew that his home and everyone in it were protected by God. I knew then without a doubt that I too had seen one of God's angels. I was blessed that night, a night I will never forget, to see the precious angel standing there, smiling back at me while protecting my children.

My stepdad didn't stay for long and as we headed back to the airport to drop him off, I felt stirred to place the letter in his bag, which I did. I wondered if he would read it, pretend he never got it or get angry with me for it, but to my surprise and delight, a few weeks later, I got an email that literally said, "Hi, thank you for your letter and I am sorry." It did not seem much but somehow it was enough for me.

Things seemed a little calmer, not everything happening at once. I felt that God was revealing things to me in a different way or with a different approach, especially as I was growing in relationship with Him. I was beginning to see beyond physical events to discern what was happening in the spiritual realm.

◆ ◆ ◆

One morning at work, my kids' child minder went to the toilet and as she went past me, I looked at her and thought she did not look well. Next thing I heard a loud bang in the toilet. I rushed through and forced my way through the door to find her collapsed on the floor, seeming to come in and out of consciousness. I could see some blood on the floor, so I picked her up, yelled to Mom to bring the car keys, my handbag, and the kids to the car quickly. As I was driving to the hospital I was praying, and I felt uneasy inside. I got her to the hospital, admitted her in and went back to work. That night at home as I was praying, I asked God to reveal what was really going on. I went to sleep that night and, in a dream, God showed me a box with a bottle in it, with things that were not good in my kids' child minder's room.

When the hospital discharged her and she came home, I went to see how she was. She came out of her room, not wanting me to enter it, and I told her that God had shown me the item she was hiding and that it was not of God. I described what God showed me and asked her what it was, where it was from and what it was for. She had worked for me for a long time and had always known that I was a Christian who deeply loved God, so this was not something new for her. She had told me she had given her life to God but was still seeing a witchdoctor for potions, as she wanted to meet a good man. After I had shared what God had shown me, she looked scared and walked away. Unknown to me then, she asked the other staff if I had entered her home while she was in the hospital for the night, which they told her I had not. She came back to see me a short while later and told me that what God had shown me scared her because what I described was exactly where and what it looked like. She asked me to forgive her and pray with her, which I did. I then explained that by bringing those things into our property it was giving the devil access, which I was against as I had given my whole home and property to God. I told her that God cared about us including her and that was why He revealed it.

Not too long after this, we had some of my relatives come over for the day and a few of them got into an argument. The argument got heated and I stepped in telling them that I did not want this in my home and if they were to carry on, they needed to leave. Well, one member got up, screamed at me and walked out. I can't even remember what they said. I let it go and that night went to bed as normal. During the night, Nathan woke up needing the toilet and came through. The kids used my bathroom ensuite, but as he came down the passage, he screamed a scream that woke me up and I felt fear all over me. He couldn't move, he just stood there screaming.

It felt like it took forever for me to get to him. I grabbed him, and he was shaking. I asked him what was wrong, and he said he saw an evil bird and it wanted to get him in the passage. I told him it was okay and we would pray. I put him in my bed and began to pray with him. He was still shaking and sobbing. I turned my bedside light on to calm him down. Deep down I knew something evil was in my home, I could feel it, and I was shaking inside. I prayed with him until he calmed down and told him that Jesus would protect us and keep us safe. I told him that I would leave him in my bed with the light on and I would go and pray and chase it away with Jesus. He hid his little four-year-old head under my sheets as I started to pray aloud and declare God's Word.

I made my way through the passage, looked in at Nicole who was still sleeping, then went into Mom's room and called her but she never responded. So, I shook her and said: "Mom, wake up, we need to pray." She got up still pretty much asleep as I led her around her bed while I was praying, and she was just mumbling. But as we got to the passage, her eyes opened wide and she began praying as hard as I was. We both saw the same thing but only described it later to each other. It looked like a bat, a very large bat of some sort hovering above the passage door frame. It was pitch black and had red-looking eyes, it had the most evil look, the kind that makes your blood feel cold in your veins. We prayed and it went. Then we got Nathan because I wanted him to see that Jesus did chase all the bad things away. I remember him clinging to me so tight, but as we made our way along the passage his little face lit up and he looked at me and said, "Jesus did chase it away." I felt relief rush over me and I thought I was going to faint. I put Nathan back to bed and Mom and I decided to sit and pray.

I was praying asking God to show me if it was something one of the employees had bought on the property from another witch doctor. But all I kept seeing was one of my sisters' names. At the end of the prayer Mom looked at me and said someone brought something into our home. We got up, prayed around the house, placing oil on the doorways as a symbolic sign of the blood of Jesus, like they did in the Bible with the lamb's blood, as we recited Psalm 91. Then we had a cup of tea because we were too wide awake to go back to sleep.

On the way to work I stopped at my sister's office and told her what had happened. I said that when I prayed, I kept seeing her name and asked what was going on. She sat staring at me quietly as I spoke, then told me that the description of the thing in my house was in the book she was reading. She wanted to show me, but I declined. It shocked both of us. I said not to read that book and if she carried on reading it, not to come visit for a while. I left trying to process what was happening. I spoke to Joh about it and he told me that because the spirit realm is a very real one, things can attach themselves to others and I had to make sure I always prayed the blood of Jesus over my home and property when people had visited, no matter who they were. My sister thought she was just reading a book, but that was not the only thing that was happening. What she had read was not godly, and when the argument happened, that spirit settled into my home.

When I spoke about this with Theunis and Deidre, they shared verses in the Bible where bad spirits would enter people and had to be cast out. God began to reveal to me the importance of what we see by way of watching, reading, what we listen to, what we focus on and what we say. We had learnt earlier on about the power of the tongue, but God was now expanding on it for me. I began to understand how things can seem harmless but are not and why we need discernment in all things. When the devil tempted Jesus in the desert, he said what was in God's Word but added something that would seem enticing. He was trying to get Jesus to act in a way that was different to God's Word.

We can watch things and at first, we feel it's not okay or alright but then afterwards we can justify why it was okay, like it's just a movie, it's not real or it's just a song, but the truth is that if we see and hear it then we will think on it. It will then be in our subconscious and that is where the danger comes in, because the temptation can become too great and we will go back to it. It affects us on a deeper level, a level we don't focus on unless we have discernment. God's Word is very clear when it says that there is power in our tongue. *What comes from our tongue?* Words! So, what we see, hear, and read becomes what we believe, follow, think, say, feel or act, instead of sticking to God's Word and His ways. I realised the importance of being aware of what the kids and I watch, listen to, and read. We love music, so I will check through what the lyrics say, as I believe that if we sing it then we are speaking it out. I know this can seem extreme to others a lot of the time, but I know that God's Word says we must have discernment regarding all things, and we must test all things with God's Word. I believe we need to test all things; we are warned that we will be deceived if we are not discerning—and it will not be blatant deception, it will be gentle, well covered, and will seem harmless and even true.

God never stops growing us and refining us, although I have learnt that it doesn't all happen at once. I will get times of learning and growing and then a time of quiet, which I feel is time for me to implement and use what I have learnt before the next learning and growing stage. I believe that God knows the time needed to learn and the time needed to absorb and use what we have been learning. I believe we need the time in order to process and use what we learn wisely.

I began to pray to God more on a daily basis, bringing more to Him. I had not yet mastered giving all things to Him nor leaving all things with Him, but definitely improved, as I heard inspirational speakers say, "I may not be where I need to be, but I thank God I am not where I used to be." It was their saying that often got me through, realising I wasn't perfect, but I was always growing.

◆ ◆ ◆

With all that I was learning at the time when Colin was away in Sudan, at night I would often lay in bed wishing that somehow, we could get out of the country. I would even lay there and create fantasies on how we would be offered the opportunity to leave Zimbabwe, and how easy it would be. That is how much I wanted us to leave and be together as a family again. After Colin's second visit home from Sudan, he told me he did not want to come back to Zimbabwe to a broken, difficult, and empty life; to a life that had very few options for improvement or change. Colin and I agreed to pray to seek God's will for our future.

Not long after he had returned to Sudan after his second visit, one of Colin's relatives, an amazing God-loving, God-fearing person, called me and invited me over to see pictures of their holiday to Australia. I agreed to go visit and saw all the wonderful pictures. As the kids and I were about to leave, they told me that they had been given details of a person who was originally from Zimbabwe and was now in Australia working as a migration agent. They shared that they had prayed and felt that Colin and I were to contact the migration agent and handed me the paper with the details on it and we said bye and left. The next time Colin and I spoke online, I told him about our visit and gave him the migration agent's details. He contacted them to see what our options were but didn't receive a reply. This went on for weeks. Colin thought there was a problem with the email having been sent from Sudan because everyone's emails were monitored, so we decided that I would try sending the email from Zimbabwe. Two weeks passed, and I hadn't received a reply either. But because we had prayed, we believed that God would reveal His will for us—we would trust Him even if Australia was not a part of God's plan for us four.

One night while I was sitting talking to Colin online, my email alert popped up, so I opened it and to my surprise, it was the migration agent. The email began with, "I don't know how I got your email because the address you used was wrong." I sent the email to Colin for him to respond to, now that we had the correct details. We saw God's hand in this and once again were humbled and amazed. Colin filled out all the paperwork and the process to find us work in Australia began. Only a few days after we had begun this process, Colin got a call from his company's head office offering him another year contract in a higher position and more than double what he was currently earning. The new contract was very attractive to him. He kept telling me that it would mean more money for us to move with, that relocating to Australia would take time if it happened, and that there was no work for him in Zimbabwe so financially it wouldn't be logical to come back.

Everything he said made sense but as I thought about it over the next few days, I felt no peace about it; it felt more like a burden. But Colin thought I was not processing it properly. I knew he had said he didn't want to come back, so my insecurities were at their highest peak again, and I was worried Colin had found someone else there. I prayed and asked others to pray for us too, yet each time I prayed the burden felt heavier, and as a deadline had been given for Colin to give an answer, we had to decide. The final night we discussed it, I told Colin that if he chose to stay on in Sudan, I would have no choice but to send him divorce papers. He was angry and I understood why, but I couldn't keep on struggling with the family divided and the weight of carrying all the stress alone when I didn't have to. I prayed hard that night that God would talk to Colin and reveal His will, because I had no idea if I would wake up to an email telling me he had accepted the offer or not. To my relief, Colin declined the offer, and told me he would be back home in May.

That week, I went to see Joh and shared that God had shown me in a dream that we were going to be moving to Australia, and that I kept seeing the month of August—just six months' away. Not long after that, Colin received an email from the migration agent. A job had come up in Katherine, a town near Darwin in the Northern Territory of Australia. After a telephonic interview, the company offered him the position. Then the nightmare of immigration paperwork began. We had been advised that the process could take up to two years, so we were ready for that. We heard nothing for a while, but a month before Colin was due to return to Zimbabwe he emailed the migration agent, who advised us that it was a struggle to get the documentation required by immigration from the company who had offered him the job. Colin told the agent to withdraw from that offer, and begin to look for another job.

This development caused me to question my dream and everything about our move. I remember standing in Joh's office telling him about my doubts. He looked at me and said, "Neena, I know you are going, even though we don't want you to leave." Later Joh asked if he and Tracey could pray with me the next morning.

The next morning in their office, they prayed over me and released me from my job as we wept together. Even as I type this, my heart is pounding and my eyes are full of tears. I can still feel the presence of God that was with us that morning.

Colin finally arrived back from Sudan. The first few days of having him home were exciting, but that soon changed. I felt he was in my way. The children were so nervous and wary of him, and he was annoyed about being back in the country and having turned down the job. Not long after, some friends invited us to join them for a holiday on a houseboat in Kariba. I had already planned a trip to England that month to visit my sister Mickey. She had moved there a few years prior, and as I wasn't sure when I would see her again, I wanted to visit her before we left Zimbabwe. Colin and I agreed that it was a good idea for him to go to Kariba for a week and do some fishing, something he loved.

Colin had only been gone two days when an email arrived from the migration agent saying a job as an orchard manager had come up, this time, in Adelaide. We set a date the following week for the interview, after Colin returned.

During the interview, Colin was asked things like his height, if he was fit, and if he could send a picture of us, and when Colin hung up the telephone, he said we shouldn't hold onto any hope for that job. Two weeks later, however, to our surprise we got a call offering Colin the job. Again, he accepted, and once again the paperwork began. We had been reminded that the process could take up to two years, but God had another plan. Just a month later we heard that our visas were approved, and could we be there by August? Shocked yet excited we said we could get there by early September. That would give us time to sort things out and find flights.

◆ ◆ ◆

After receiving the call to say that Colin had the job, we began to let our family know that we were planning to move. This was especially important to Dad, as by now I was his only child left in Zimbabwe who checked on him, made sure he had all he needed, and was okay. Since the divorce, Dad had not had much contact with my half siblings, and now he and his wife were also separated. Dad kept saying that he would stay in Zimbabwe, but I knew this wasn't an option. Dad didn't do well with the lack of food, money, water, electricity, and work, let alone the racial contempt in Zimbabwe. I knew that he would not live long if I left him there. After speaking to Mickey in the United Kingdom, we discussed the possibility of Dad joining her there. We agreed, but we had very little time to organise things for Dad.

That night as we sat around his bar, I told him we had no choice but to sell his house. It was not an easy conversation, nor a good one. Dad screamed and ranted at me, telling me how he did not want to leave, how he had worked his whole life to pay for that house. He was so angry that I was just going to sell it and move him far away. I explained as best I could why we needed to get him to England, and when we left that night, he was still angry but knew the house had to be sold.

I spent most of that night in prayer as I did not want to arrange for Dad to go to England if it was not part of God's plan. The next morning, I woke up feeling peaceful. I called an estate agent and spoke to them about selling Dad's house, and within an hour we met to have the house evaluated. Dad had an idea of the price he wanted for the house, and to our surprise they valued it higher. Three days later, I got a call from the agent advising me that they had a buyer.

The amazing thing is, that nine months earlier, Dad had gone to South Africa and the United Kingdom to visit relatives and friends, and to see Mickey. While he was away, we decided to surprise him and renovate his house. He lived alone by then, and was no longer able to maintain the property. Every night after work, Mom and I would go to the house with the kids in tow and work, scrubbing walls and floors, repainting, fixing up the garden, and more. We also employed people to continue the renovation during the day while I was at work. We got it all completed the day before he arrived home.

Dad was not very thankful for the surprise; instead he was angry. Even so, I look back now and see how God had already put His plan into action. Because we had done so much work, the house was ready to be viewed and sold as soon as the time came.

Dad was eligible to apply for a United Kingdom ancestry visa, so I got that underway. The process in Zimbabwe at the time, was that you had to go to the office where applications were submitted, join a queue to get the appropriate form, then join another queue to get a date to submit your application. These two processes normally took at least a few days but I was able to get both done on the same day. That night I got all the paperwork filled out, and the next day had copies of his official documents certified. Dad came with me the following day to get his fingerprints and photo taken, and to submit the application. We arrived to long queues, which infuriated Dad because he hates waiting, but eventually we reached the front and got everything done and submitted. We were advised that we would have an answer in the next six months. *Six months!* My jaw hit the floor. We would be well on our way to Australia before then. I decided I would have to make arrangements for Dad in case he had to stay behind on his own for a while.

The very next night, however, I got a message from the visa company advising me there was an envelope for me to collect. Colin and I agreed not to tell anyone, as I was feeling sick to the stomach, thinking I had made an error with the application, or that something else was wrong. That night I could not sleep. I had signed the agreement of sale for Dad's house just two days earlier. Thoughts like, *Where is Dad going to live?* plagued my mind throughout the long hours of the night.

When morning came, I got the kids ready, dropped them at school, and Colin and I made our way back to the visa office. There was already a long queue when I arrived, so Colin waited in the car. Sitting in the queue, I was praying so hard for God to calm me down, when one of the staff came over to me to collect the slip of paper I had with a reference number on it. Bear in mind that I was the only white person in the queue at this point. When the man looked at the date on the slip of paper and saw it was only just over twenty-four hours since we had submitted the application, he began to mock me and laugh at me. I remember trying to block him out and not be rude. He asked me if I thought the visa had been granted? Others were staring at me now, but I looked at him and said, "Yes." I was sure it had.

Deep inside I was asking God to back me up; I was throwing out my fleece here and I needed Him to keep it dry. The man laughed so hard that Colin even lowered his window to hear what was going on. After disappearing for half an hour, the man returned. He handed envelopes to the others who were in line, then turned to me asking what made me think the visa was in the envelope? I replied, "Because I prayed, and I know the God I serve." Again, he laughed and told me that I had to open it in front of him and the other people there because he was sure I was never going to leave Zimbabwe. I slowly peeled the envelope open, shaking like a leaf. Pulling out the passport which had been left open, I turned it over, and there was an ancestry visa for Dad! The man's and everyone else's jaws were wide open, and I burst into a sob. As I started to run towards Colin, the man shouted to me that the God I serve is a good God.

Colin, seeing me sobbing, was sure it was bad news, but as I got close to him, I said, "We got it, we got it!" We drove straight to see Dad. I held his passport up and said, "Dad, we got it, you are going to the UK!" Within one week we had sold his house, got more money for it than we expected, and the application for the visa had been submitted and approved! God was blowing my mind in this season of transition, teaching me I was not only to pray to Him, I was to trust Him with the things I was praying for. Trust had never come easily to me; even now I have to remind myself of this whenever I feel the need to be in control.

I began the process of packing up two homes and selling items. Nothing was straightforward, and truthfully, I was falling apart trying to deal with everything. I was barely holding it together and felt as if I was on the brink of a nervous breakdown. There were days where it seemed I could deal with anything and then others where I could barely face breakfast. I had reached the end of myself; I was not in control, God was. He was who I needed, and I clung to Him, even if it was by my nails on the very hem of His garment. It was then that I learnt that His Word is true—God never leaves us, and He is truly strong even when we are weak.

Apart from Colin's job, we had nothing else in place for our arrival in Australia. We had been trying to look for somewhere to live in South Adelaide, but we couldn't find anything. With only a week to go before we left, we were becoming increasingly concerned. But then God showed us He had all the details sorted, and we received an email advising us of a house we could rent. Things were being moulded by God's hand. It seemed that it was when we realised we had no control, and chose to surrender our plans and trust the Lord, that we then saw God working.

With everything going on, time seemed to go so fast, and before we knew it, we were at the airport saying goodbye to the people we loved so much and with whom I had shared my life for nearly thirty years. As we sat outside with them all, we laughed and acted like it was not going to happen. Then, just before we were to go through to the departure lounge, one of my abusers, who I had tried to talk to years back, asked to speak to me in private. We walked a short distance away from the crowd, then he looked at me and said that what he did to me was terrible; he was sorry and asked me to forgive him. I was unprepared for this, but I gladly forgave him and was thankful that God had used the years in between to bring us both to a place of healing. Every step God had taken me on to this point had grown me and freed me. I had already learnt that forgiveness was not an admission that the other person or what they had done was okay, but that in forgiving and releasing the person and situation into God's hands, I was being set free from the bondage.

The time came and we lined up and began our goodbyes, fighting back the sobs as we kissed and hugged each person. I still feel the pain in my heart now as I write about it. My heart hurt so much, I wished I could have taken it out of my body. When Theunis and Deidre said goodbye, they said God had to move us away from those we love in order to use us, just like Abraham in the Bible. It did not make sense to me then, but it was similar to what Joh and Tracey had said too.

We walked through the terminal, looking back every few steps and waving, blowing kisses, just not knowing when or if we would see everyone again. We were filled with both excitement and fear as we set out for a new country, one we had never seen before.

STEP OUT OF THE WILDERNESS

Take a moment to sit with the Holy Spirit. What situations have you been viewing only through your physical eyes? Invite Him to open your eyes to see what is really going on in those places. Is there any action you sense Him showing you to take? In what areas is unforgiveness holding you back from stepping into a new season? Invite the Holy Spirit to empower you to forgive and show you if any action is required to reflect this internal posture of surrender.

CHAPTER EIGHT

He uncovers deep things out of darkness, and brings the shadow of death to light.
Job 12 v 22

After multiple delays with our flights, we finally arrived late at night in our new homeland. It was hard to believe as we landed that it was only three and a half months earlier that Colin had accepted the job offer in Australia. Colin's boss was at the airport to collect us, and as we made the forty-five-minute drive from Adelaide airport to a little town outside the city, we quietly observed the surroundings. Colin was making conversation with his new employer when the topic of drink-driving came up. "It doesn't happen much in Australia," we were told. But within minutes of that conversation, the vehicle in front of us swerved all over the road and suddenly hit a tree! We were surprised that Colin's boss didn't stop to check on the driver, but simply laughed and commented that the tree the driver hit was right in front of the police station.

Entering the driveway of our new house, everything was dark and it was such a cold night. As we opened the front door the kids said to us, "There are no lights. We thought this was going to be better here." Colin's boss smiled as he went over to a switch and turned a light on. He had arranged the essentials for the house, which we appreciated, as we arrived with only six suitcases filled with clothes and a few treasured items like photos. He told Colin that he would give him a week to get settled. Our first goal was to purchase a car.

The next morning, a Sunday, we woke up and made our way outside, then wandered around the little town to find the supermarket. We soon decided to only buy milk and bread, as we were overwhelmed by the variety—there were more than five brands of bread and milk alone to choose from! This was amazing to us. Not knowing which one to choose, we turned to ask a lady which brands were best. Well, she gave us a very strange look, pointed at one of each, and walked away. We made our way home, realising that not everyone was as friendly as we had expected.

On the Monday morning, we got a ride into Adelaide and were dropped off on a very long street with car dealerships all the way along it. To our shock the price we had sold all our vehicles for in Zimbabwe, couldn't even buy us one vehicle in Australia. We were disheartened and worried as we headed back to our new town, as we needed a vehicle for Colin to get to work the following week.

That night we walked to the supermarket once again to get supplies for dinner. Before walking home, we sat down on a bench outside the supermarket for a while, when we noticed a single cab truck (known as a 'Ute' in Australia) drive past with a 'for sale' sign on it, along with a phone number. Colin called the number right away, looked over the vehicle, and bought it. Now in Zimbabwe, we could drive with all four of us in the front, so that's what we did. We four hopped into the vehicle and drove to the next big town to have a look around. Somehow, we made a turn into what looked like a road entrance but wasn't, and ended up blocking the main road as traffic came towards us. We noticed we were getting strange looks, and kept looking out for police lights as we manoeuvred our way off the road. When Colin went to work the following Monday and he shared what had happened, he was told that we weren't allowed to have four of us in the front. That's when we realised we would also need a car—one that we could all fit in. We added it to the long list of items we needed.

Within a week we had a bank account sorted out, along with telephone and internet so we could message everyone at home to let them know we had arrived safely. We were blessed as the school was right over our back fence, so I could easily walk the children to school and home again. In time I found a second-hand vehicle to use with the kids, but that turned out to be a big mistake. It cost so much to run and needed a lot of work done, which we could not afford. Now, with the kids settled in their new school, I found myself alone at home all day, short of money, unable to go out, and since I didn't have friends, there wasn't much for me to do but clean the house and tend to the garden, which was very small. It was not an easy time.

Colin wasn't happy either. There were huge differences in the way things were done in Australia in comparison to Zimbabwe, and it turned out that his employer was not that nice to work for. Colin would come home every day in a terrible mood, which was made worse knowing he was obligated to stay there for four years. We had no option but to put up with the situation, as we didn't want to risk being sent back to Zimbabwe. Within a few weeks of arriving, we were already questioning why we moved.

◆ ◆ ◆

With all the busyness of moving and getting re-established, the distance that had grown between us when Colin worked in Sudan was back. As normal life resumed, so too did the old dynamics of our relationship. But in some ways, it was more intense as we only had each other; it was even more of a struggle to re-unite our family when we were the only focus. I needed to find work but couldn't because I didn't have any Australian qualifications. This put further pressure on our relationship as Colin had to work weekends in order to cover our living expenses. If it rained, he couldn't work, and that meant he didn't get paid. Arguments over both of our work situations became more and more frequent.

The kids were also finding it hard to settle in. They were being teased in school because of their accents and the way different words were pronounced in Australia, like 'mum' instead of 'mom'. As I couldn't find work, I volunteered in the school to do reading in class when I was needed. I tried to introduce myself to a few parents but as soon as I spoke and they heard my accent, they would literally walk away. When I went to pick the kids up, I just sat alone, quietly, not wanting to approach anyone after my previous experiences.

As the days went on, I struggled more and more. All I could think of was our family and friends back in Zimbabwe, who I seldom heard from unless they needed something from me. This increased my sense of isolation. I felt like I had never really mattered to them, that I was 'out of sight, out of mind'. Old hurts and questions began to rise in me again, and I wondered if I would ever be free from them.

I had so many questions for God, like: *Why did you do this to us? Why did you move us, and now we are no better off? In fact, why are we worse off?* We had come to Australia to find a better life but instead found ourselves struggling financially, emotionally, and spiritually. We had no friends or family. There didn't seem to be a church in the area, and we had no idea how we could form connections. Without the appropriate qualifications I was left feeling powerless to help with our finances. I couldn't even look at doing a course to enable me to find a job because we could not afford it.

The emails from family back home about their struggles increased my sense of helplessness. At least when I was there, I could help them, pray with them, and be there as a support for them. Now I was watching them all fall apart from a distance, and I was worried they would lose their grip on God too. Little did I know that Colin was having similar arguments with God in his prayer time, but we were so distant with each other that we were not really sharing any of it.

As each day passed, I cried out to God, literally cried, daily, for months on end. I would sit at our lounge window where the sun shone through, and read the Bible, trying to find God and His will amongst my chaos and pain. One morning I turned on the television and found a channel with sermons on it. As I watched, it was as if the speakers were there just to talk to me. I remember sitting there and feeling a spark of hope rising in me. As I read the verses they gave, I began to see that once again I had taken control and was focusing on everything that was going on, rather than on God. I was reminded of the lessons I had begun to learn in the months leading to us moving from Zimbabwe. I remember sitting there by the window wondering why God loved me when I so easily forgot what He had begun in me, and the lessons He had shown me.

The Holy Spirit impressed upon me to read the scripture where, after Jesus was crucified, the disciples decided to go back to fishing. I was shocked. I had never really understood the significance of that moment. The disciples had walked with Jesus day in and day out, witnessing miracles and teachings that amaze us even today, yet as soon as He was gone, not even that was enough to keep them following in His footsteps. I began to realise how important the Holy Spirit really is, something I had not realised properly before. Our own strength is not adequate.

As I read through these verses, I could hear God talking. The Holy Spirit was leading me, and His Word felt alive again to me. I began to pray and ask God for His direction, believing that He brought us to Australia, and that He had a plan for us. Part of that plan, I believed, was to help get our wider family to Australia or out of Zimbabwe. But I also sensed it was bigger than that, that we would also help others struggling back in Zimbabwe, the poor. Excitement returned and I started to feel less depressed. With renewed expectation I began to pray for the restoration of my marriage, and God opened my eyes to the things that we needed to work through. I made the most of all the time I had alone at home to pray and seek God for direction for every area of our lives. And, I kept believing for a job so I could contribute to our finances.

Our finances constantly pressed on me. The rainy season had begun, and Colin was being sent home more frequently, which meant money got tighter and tighter. The home that had been arranged for us was proving unsuitable for a number of reasons, and Colin and I discussed moving house. We had no idea how we could make that happen as we had no furniture and no money for a rent deposit, but for the first time in a long time, we prayed together, asking God for direction about where we were to live and the timing of applying for our permanent residency.

One week it rained a few days in a row and with Colin at home, we decided to get into serious prayer together. We lay on the floor in our loungeroom, and began to pray. We prayed for what felt like minutes but turned out to be hours, and as we prayed, we wept to God, opening up our hearts fully to Him.

Soon it was time to get the kids from school. It was a Wednesday, and as we had enrolled Nathan in an Australian football team for children, we got ready and went to the field, or as they call it in Australia, the 'oval'. We watched Nathan as he ran around not really interested. The coach said something about throwing grass in the wind to show the direction of the wind, or something along those lines, so Nathan ran around tearing grass and throwing it in the air and laughing. We decided at that point that this was probably not going to work. We had wanted Nathan to play sport so we could meet other families, but that wasn't working either.

Defeated, we made our way home, where all we had to eat was a few slices of bread, which we gave to the children. Colin and I would make do with a hot drink. As I was making the coffee, there was a knock at the door. I slowly peeled the lace from the window and peeped out, still feeling unsafe about being in a house with no bars on the windows or doors. Seeing a lady standing there, I opened the door and we greeted each other. After introducing herself, she explained that she had heard through the school that we were from Africa, and as they had connections with people in South Africa, they thought they would reach out to us. She explained that they owned a bakery and every night they had leftovers, and she hoped we did not take offense to her bringing a box of leftovers for us. I stood there fighting back tears, trying to speak normally as I thankfully accepted the box. She told me they wanted to have us over to their house for lunch on Saturday, and gave me her address before leaving.

I walked through to the kitchen just as Colin was asking who it was, when he saw me holding the box, with tears streaming down my face. He jumped up and looked in the box as I put it on the counter. I repeated what the lady had said, and with tears in our eyes we looked up to the heavens with such gratitude and thankfulness. You see, the food in that box was enough to feed the four or us for the next week and a half! We were so emotional and thankful we could not speak but were praising God in our hearts. We explained to the kids what had just happened and how God had answered our prayers from earlier that day.

Saturday came, and we went to lunch but got lost and arrived very late. I hadn't taken the woman's phone number, so could not call to ask directions. We arrived at their door very embarrassed, and explained why we were so late as we sat with them around the table. They laughed and said it was fine, that they had eaten but we should eat. There was so much amazing food on the table! As we sat together, they explained their affiliation with South Africa—they were in a church which was connected to a missionary there. I can't tell you the joy in my heart that we had just met Christians, whose children went to our kids' school too! I wanted to jump up, dance, and scream praise to God.

As the afternoon turned to evening, we were still sitting around when the lady asked if we enjoyed the box of food, to which I got all emotional and shared how that day there was nothing left in the house and we had asked God to help and guide us, then she arrived that night with the box. She in turn got tears in her eyes as she said that when she knocked on the door, it was the third time she had come to the house that night. She told us that she was so nervous about coming, and had prayed too, wondering if she was supposed to bring the box to us. She said that even after coming to our door twice before, God led her to come back again. As we left that night, this family gave us another box of food, something they did for us for the next few years. As time went on, we got to bless others with the food in the box too!

◆ ◆ ◆

Eventually we managed to save for a deposit on a rental house and found one which we were interested in, but it fell through. Because we were new in Australia and had no references or anyone to stand as guarantor for us, it made applying for a rental a little difficult. I explained to the agent why we wanted to leave the house we were in. The agent was a wonderful lady who truly wanted to help us get into another home. She called me soon after to say she had another house coming up for rent and wanted to show me. I went to look at the house, and it was perfect. That afternoon I prayed that if it was God's will, He would open the door for us, and if not, to close it.

Around the same time, we had applied to the Immigration Department of Australia for permanent residence. This was a long process. I recall one Wednesday night, when we got a call from our migration agent saying that we had to have new medicals done, and that they wanted them by the following Tuesday or they would be cancelling the visas we were on and sending us back to Zimbabwe. Confused and frustrated, that night in bed Colin and I prayed that God's will be done; we believed God opened doors for us to move to Australia and that it wasn't just to send us back.

The next morning, I called to make an appointment for our medicals and was told we could go in the next day for the chest x-rays, but that the only available appointment for the full medical test was in two weeks. When I explained our situation, the lady said she could not help. After praying, I called Colin and told him I had booked the date in two weeks, thinking that if I gave the immigration a booked date, they might give us some time. Colin took the next day off work, and we made our first trip to Adelaide, where we parked the car and walked to the radiology centre for our x-rays. When they were done, we sat down to wait for the films. Soon someone asked what we were waiting for, and when we replied, they explained that they had already electronically sent the x-rays to the doctor we would be seeing for the medical. Surprised, as we never had this technology at home, we called the medical centre to check they had received the x-rays and they had, so I asked if there had been any cancellations. Unfortunately there were none, but as I was talking to the person on the phone, they noticed that our address was nearly an hour out of Adelaide. If we were willing to stay in Adelaide for the day, the lady said, then they would squeeze us in for the medical. I almost screamed my yes down the phone!

With all our tests done, there was nothing to do but wait. The deadline of Tuesday came, and we heard nothing from immigration during the day. But late that evening when the kids were watching cartoons and I was getting ready to have a bath, I heard Colin's mobile phone ring. Next thing, the bathroom door opened and Colin just stood there with the phone to his ear as he said "thank you" and hung up. Immigration had approved our permanent residence!

It felt like a weight had been lifted off our shoulders. We could not stop thanking God that night for ensuring our future in Australia was permanent. Our newfound security brought much joy to our home. We were growing closer to God and growing as a family too, learning that the four of us were blessed to have each other.

◆ ◆ ◆

Now that we could put our roots down, it was time to establish wider connections. We had been visiting our new friends' church, but felt it was not where we were to be, so began looking for a Hillsong Church, as that was what we had watched on television in Zimbabwe. We reached out, and were told there was no Hillsong church in Adelaide but they gave us the name of a church that was similar, called Paradise Church. So, we decided that we would go there the following Sunday and see what it was like.

The moment we walked in, we felt that we had arrived home. It was a huge church, but we knew it was where we should be. All four of us had such a sense of home when we were in the church, a peace that we couldn't explain, and a joy. We could not afford to go every weekend as it was a long way, and the car we had was very expensive to run, so we decided we would only go once a month and if we had extra money, then twice. But it was always worth it.

◆ ◆ ◆

Not long before we had applied for our permanent residency, we had begun looking to buy a smaller car that was more economical and easier to service. We had found a small Hyundai which we were very interested in buying, but as we were not permanent residents yet, we were unable to get a loan. We prayed about this, and asked God that if it was His will that again He would open doors or close them. The following week, the salesman we were dealing with called and said that if we paid a five-hundred-dollar deposit, they would hold the vehicle. That was too risky for us to put down, I thought, as it was non-refundable and at that stage, we did not know how long it would be before we got our permanent visa (or if we would get it at all). Unsure of what to do at this point, we said we would call him back soon with a decision.

The week our permanent visas were approved, we had to take our passports to the immigration office to get the visas put in them. Once that was done, we were advised to register with Medicare. We had no idea what this meant, but since we were in Adelaide, we said yes and went to the Medicare office, thinking it was all part of the visa requirement and that I wanted to get everything done as soon as possible.

At the Medicare office we were sat down and asked questions as our answers were entered into the computer. We were then asked to sign a few forms before being handed a temporary card. Surprised, we asked what the card was for? The Medicare officer explained that it was to help cover the cost of doctor's visits and medications in some instances, and hospital if needed, especially for the kids. Our mouths must have been hanging wide open, because the person helping us asked what was wrong. We explained how much this touched us, as in Zimbabwe we had no help from the government like this. We were further surprised when they explained that we now needed to register with Centrelink, and that we would get fortnightly assistance from the government for living expenses for the kids. My mind was spinning at this point. I could not comprehend how, overnight, we went from financially struggling to being so blessed.

It had been a condition of our temporary visa that we have private insurance, but at this point, we decided we no longer needed it. The health cover was costing us just over five hundred dollars a month—and now we were free to cancel it, as Medicare covered so much, and we seldom got sick.

It was in the week we were doing all of this, that the salesman from the car company called. We told him we had just been granted our permanent visa, and organised to meet him. When he worked through the paperwork for the car loan, he advised us that the monthly payment would be just over five hundred dollars a month. I could not believe it! Our repayments would be just three dollars more than our health insurance had cost, which meant we could afford to get the car! The salesman submitted the loan application, and a few days later called us with the good news it had been approved.

We still could not afford to go on long trips, but we could go to church more than once a month, and every time we went, God revealed more of Himself to us and grew our faith. He even put it on other people's hearts at the church to bless us with money, which they felt God wanted us to use to get to church more often. Being such a big church, God taught us we were going there for Him, to meet with Him, not for the people or the atmosphere. It was a wonderful time of growing and deepening our relationship with Him.

◆ ◆ ◆

It was an added blessing when we found we had been approved to move into the new house I had looked at with the agent, but as our moving day approached, I was concerned about our need for furniture. Some friends I was speaking to mentioned a couple who were retiring to another town, and were selling their house and all their furniture. I called the phone number I was given and organised to go with a friend to look at the furniture. There were a couple of items I said I would like, and asked the couple to let me know a price. I was hoping we could pay the items off over the next few weeks, before we moved into the house. While I was there, we got talking, and I told them where we had come from and a little about us. It was a lovely conversation.

A few days later we got a call from the couple asking us to come and see them. After a brief chat, they told us they no longer wanted to sell the items to us. My heart dropped, but then they went on to say they wanted to give us the items we had planned to buy from them—and more! At first, I thought I was hearing things, and asked if they were sure, as we did not expect that at all. They assured us they did and would call us when it was ready to collect.

The smiles on their faces, so full of genuine love and concern, are a picture I will never forget. They blessed us with beds for all of us, bedside tables, plates, glasses, cutlery, linen, and more, more than we ever imagined. We were humbled that yet again God had used strangers to touch our lives. The week we were moving into the new house, the couple's daughter and son-in-law arrived with a dining room suite for us as well! We moved into our new house, which was bigger than the last, cheaper in rent, and we had all the furniture and items we needed to make it home! As I look back, it still blows my mind and humbles me to see all God had done.

But that was not all. God had plans for work for me too. One day when I was volunteering at the kids' school, I was told that a job opening had come up at another school in the area. I sent my resume in, had an interview, and got a part-time job. God had used my volunteer work to open a door of employment for me! With the financial pressure eased, we could explore our region a little, and buy Christmas and birthday presents—all things we had gone without. But more than that, with every act of provision, we were learning more about who God was, and that no matter what, our choices need to be founded on Him each day. We had begun our journey to Australia with no idea of the bigger picture that God could see. Now, we had begun to make our home in our new land.

STEP OUT OF THE WILDERNESS

In what area of your life do you most need to experience a breakthrough? Spend some time prayerfully seeking the Lord. What promise is He giving you to stand on? Commit to speak that promise out every day and ask Him to show you what your part is in seeing it come to fruition.

CHAPTER NINE

Being confident of this very thing, that He who has begun a good work in you will complete it until the day of Jesus Christ.
Philippians 1 v 6

Not long after we moved to Australia, God began challenging me that there should be nothing hidden from Colin about me. I didn't think I was hiding anything, but then I began to have dreams about some of the abuse I had endured as a child. I could see the face of one of the perpetrators so clearly. I prayed and prayed, unsure of what was going on. I thought I had dealt with my abuse, until one day when I felt God ask me to assess how I saw and felt about myself. As I did this, an intense pain emerged from deep within. I wanted to hide, and in that moment, I realised that I still felt guilty, as if I was to blame and a part of me was dirty. The only way I can describe what I felt, is that I had a black dirty area inside of me. I began to work through it in prayer daily, but I was too scared to talk to Colin about it in case he also thought I caused it and was dirty. That's when God told me it was time to bring it all out of the dark.

I felt sick in my stomach, knowing that I needed to tell Colin. That night when the kids were sleeping, I asked Colin if we could have a talk. He came into the room and I told him about the dream I kept having. Colin told me I had never actually told him about the abuse, only that it had happened, which confirmed what God had said about still having hidden areas of my life. I explained my reasons for not telling Colin before, and through many tears finally told him everything. It was a hard conversation. Colin got so angry with what he heard, but I kept asking him to forgive my abusers as I had. I remember the house was always so cold, but that night it felt freezing. Eventually we went to sleep.

The next morning I woke up feeling more open to Colin, but the feeling of dirtiness remained. *Did Colin now also see me as dirty?* That night after the kids went to bed, Colin and I had another discussion. He told me he didn't see me any differently, which was a relief. I hoped it was all dealt with once and for all.

We had just moved into our new house when the dreams about my abuser started happening again. I asked God why I was having these dreams. I desperately wanted to be clean and whole, but the recurring dreams just left me feeling even more dirty. In my mind, I replayed what I had shared with Colin to see if I had lied, twisted anything, or left anything out. I thought that by having our talk and bringing the abuse into the light, I should have felt clean and free.

I began speaking to the Lord about this, and He led me to the scripture that says, "as we judge others, so we will be judged." I sought God about why He had shown me this, and God reminded me of my reaction when I heard that a man who abused me had died in a motorbike accident. I could see it play out as if I was watching a film. I had run out on to the veranda of the house we had lived in when I was younger, looked up to the heavens, and celebrated, believing that justice had been served for me.

Now, I felt like the worst person on the planet as I realised that as I had judged, I was to be judged. I fell to my knees in our back garden, weeping, asking God to forgive me, and I felt the Holy Spirit prompt me to forgive that man. I knew that when I gave my life to God and invited Jesus in, I was saved, and that when I repented, I was forgiven. But there are times when God brings up things that we still need to work through, because He does not want us to be bound or held back because of what has happened. He knows when something within us is causing us to withhold from others and from Him, and He wants to free us from it.

Now I could see that I pushed this man to the back of my mind because I decided as a little girl that by him dying, God had sorted him out for me.

But my understanding was contorted and wrong. Before I had received apologies for my abuse, one of my abusers suffered for years and had many terrible experiences. I would sometimes think that was what they were owed for what they did to me. God reminded me of these thoughts too. What God was teaching me, was not that He was about to send me to hell and never forgive me, but rather that I had a wrong picture of God. The same God who I loved and who loved me, loved *everyone*, including my abusers. God was sharing His heart with me, a heart that loves unconditionally and wanted me, and each of us, to be close to Him so that we in turn can learn how to love like Him.

By all that I had said and thought, I was in effect saying that I was better than others, that God would rather punish people for their sins than redeem them. This is not the truth. I realised that as long as I held on to these feelings, I would never truly get close to Colin because I still had a wrong opinion of men. I saw that I was making biased choices in raising Nathan that could affect him and his life negatively. Likewise in raising Nicole—my choices would influence her relationships with males. If I held onto my wrong beliefs, we would be robbed of the fullness that God had for us both individually and as a family.

I knew that only the Lord is given the right to judge, and that is because He judges without prejudice. Our human judgment is not like that—we are always biased. I needed to face this judgemental spirit, bind it, and be loosed of it in order to grow closer to God, my husband, and my children, as well as to be an example to my children. I needed to break it off me so that I could be freed of it.

As I prayed on this, I asked God to send me someone with similar experiences who could help me. One day at church, a well-known female speaker shared her story of abuse. Afterwards I wanted to talk to her to ask how she got rid of the dirty, black feeling of darkness. I walked down the stairs in a hurry, worried I would miss her, and raced over to where she was standing to ask my question. I will never forget it—the speaker looked at me and said she was sorry but she couldn't help me. I walked away that day filled with anger, thinking, *You just stood up there and preached, and that was all you could give me?* When I told Colin her response, he looked at me and said, "Maybe God wants to do this one with you alone." And that was exactly what God did.

God sometimes uses other people to guide us, but at other times it just needs to be between you and the Holy Spirit. Sometimes God will even resolve something in us without ever revealing the root of the issue, because He knows that what is binding us up just needs to be broken off us or let go of. His method is always the best.

As I got alone with God, He reminded me of a time in Zimbabwe when I was approached at a gathering one day by a person who asked my forgiveness for the things they had done to me as a baby. I said I forgave them, but I had never really processed it. As I remembered this, I was amazed that even back then God was tearing down my walls, the walls that blocked Him and others out. I wanted so desperately to be loved and be worthy, yet I kept everyone at a certain distance to stay safe. Now, I released those people, binding the spirits that had attached to me, and loosing myself and others of it all. I truly chose to forgive them that day, all of them, for everything—even the things only God knew had happened to me. I chose to forgive myself too, and felt a weight lifting off my shoulders.

The next morning when I woke up, for the first time in my life, I felt clean inside, no more blackness. That may sound simple, but it was not; it had taken a process to bring me to that place. But still, it was a new day for me with God. My prayer life deepened, and my love for others became more genuine. I wanted to share the love God had shown me with others, and to walk alongside them as they allowed God to do what was needed in their life.

Around this time, God used me to encourage a family with similar circumstances involving abuse. What a blessing it was to see them experience the same freedom I had! This is why the process of healing is so important—it enables us to be used in the lives of others; to be God's hands and feet on this earth.

God continued to stir me to come alongside people, particularly by sharing words with them. At first, most of these opportunities came during my volunteer work. I would simply share what I felt God was saying during the course of our conversations. Many times, I felt nervous or not want to say certain things because I was sure it would anger people. When I leant on my own wisdom, it fell apart terribly. But amazingly, when I shared what God led me to, people always told me that they appreciated how I spoke the truth with them. Sometimes, God would even stir me to say or share things with people I had only met briefly. As I grew in my understanding and sensitivity to the truth that it was all about Him, not me, I began to see Him move powerfully.

God speaking to others through me made me feel worthier than I could ever explain—worthy in that God saw He could trust me, because I longed to hear Him say, "Oh, good and faithful servant of mine, I am pleased with you." Every time I obeyed God, that was the feeling I got deep in my heart—that God was smiling, and would one day say those words to me. Finally, I felt like life was on track and I was doing what I was called to do.

◆ ◆ ◆

Then, sickness began to hit our family hard. By now we had been in Australia for three years. During this time, we had experienced better health than ever. This year, however, we all seemed to keep getting the flu, and were sicker than we had been in a very long time. Drawing on past experience, I sought God to see if we were doing anything that was creating a break in our protection. I searched long and hard and asked but heard nothing. Things seemed to get worse. Nicole suffered from really bad colds, flu and allergies, and I had been struggling with my left side going numb often. I only needed to sit for five minutes and my leg and arm would go numb. I was sure it was a pinched nerve, so I went to a chiropractor, but it never helped.

I also began seeing a number of black spots in my left eye and I was getting severe headaches, so I thought I needed new glasses. I went to see the optometrist, who referred me to a specialist. I went from specialist to specialist, five to be precise—each unwilling to tell us exactly what they thought or found. These visits were not covered by Medicare, and we no longer had health insurance, although that probably wouldn't have covered it anyway. Finally, we demanded the specialist give us an answer. He told me that all the specialists I had seen agreed that I had a very rare eye disease, and that I could possibly lose my sight in my left eye. In the process of having all the different tests, doctors also found a lump in my left breast.

Meanwhile, Nathan was suffering from severe earaches, allergies, and what I thought were extremely bad 'growing pains'. I would have to sit with him for hours at night, rubbing his legs. Nicole had experienced this as well, though it didn't last as long. I was sure it was normal, so I just did my best to make sure Nathan was getting enough calcium and magnesium, and so on.

Then one Saturday he was playing outside with Nicole, learning how to roller skate, when he fell. He screamed, so I ran out to see what had happened, then took him inside and put a cold pack on his leg where it hurt. After a few minutes, he got up and went outside again, but within twenty minutes, he made his way back in. I say 'made his way', but in reality, he was crawling towards me, sobbing that his legs were too painful to stand up. I felt worried now, so I lay him on the couch and put a cold pack on his legs again, but the pain was getting worse. Within an hour, he was flushed in the face and his temperature was high. Colin and I decided to call the doctor for an appointment, but they were all fully booked so we made an appointment for Monday and gave him Panadol to manage his pain and temperature.

I got no sleep that night. Nathan's temperature reached 40^0 C and he did not want to eat or drink. I lay in the lounge with him, and in the early hours of the morning, after placing him in a cool bath to get his temperature down but with no success, we rushed him to the emergency department at the local hospital where the staff checked him over. As it was a Sunday, no one was available to take an x-ray unless it was an emergency, and they felt Nathan was not an emergency case. They told us he probably had a viral bug which he would get over in a few days, and that we should carry on giving pain relief every two hours.

I knew something was not right. Our kids never played up or acted sick, ever. But we could do nothing else, so we went home. But by that afternoon,

Nathan's temperature had not lowered, even with two medications. More worried than before, we rushed him to a larger hospital in the next town, where we received similar advice—the doctors were sure he would be over it in three days. We left again with a little boy who was crying, had no energy, and could not walk so we had to carry him everywhere.

That night his temperature climbed towards 42° C. Knowing this meant possible convulsions or worse, I called the newly-implemented health line. As I went through Nathan's symptoms and explained the advice we had received, the nurse told me I needed to hang up and get Nathan to the Women's and Children's Hospital in Adelaide immediately. I woke Colin and quickly we made our way into Adelaide. The entire drive, my little boy cried about how sore he was, and all I could say was *sorry*. By this point, he could put no weight at all on his feet or legs, and if he tried, he just screamed. For a few days he had not wanted to eat; it was as if we could see him losing weight before our eyes.

Arriving at the emergency department of the Women's and Children's Hospital, we explained what was happening, then took a seat in the waiting room and began to fill out the paperwork. Thankfully, Nathan's crying and our attempts to comfort him caught the attention of a doctor, who took one look at Nathan, picked him up, and told us to follow him. He was moving fairly fast, and I was almost jogging to keep up.

Nathan was admitted immediately and as soon as they took his temperature, the doctor told the nurses to get a drip into him and to get his temperature down. The nurses applied numbing gel in various areas to insert a cannula, but as Nathan was dehydrated and his veins had collapsed, they had to insert it in an area where there was no numbing gel, which made Nathan scream.

The doctors started Nathan on a broad-spectrum antibiotic as they ran further tests, but because his condition was getting worse, they wanted to administer the medication through the cannula. By now the nurses realised the cannula was not inserted correctly, and as a result, Nathan's arm was swelling. Another nurse came to reinsert the cannula, but it snapped off in his arm. The doctor then came to get that out and put a new one in. I could not handle seeing my little boy going through all this. The doctor left, and a few minutes later called to say he was taking Nathan to theatre to insert a PICC line. I then went in to the theatre to hold Nathan still as they inserted the line into a main artery to his heart, with a heart surgeon on standby in case it went wrong. You can imagine the state I was in while trying to hold it together for my little one.

Once the PICC line was inserted, the medication was given. Nathan cried and said it was burning his heart, which we had known would happen. Nathan stayed in hospital for three weeks, during which time he was diagnosed with a bone infection and disease. The doctors explained this was caused by Nathan's bones absorbing the mucus from his allergies to pollen. The bone in his foot had disintegrated to a point that if Nathan put any weight on it, it would cause irreversible damage. They told us that if we had left Nathan a few hours longer before bringing him to hospital, we would have been burying him.

Finally, Nathan was discharged from hospital and we went home. His foot was in a cast that went halfway up his leg, and he had to use crutches. The nurses and physiotherapist said that the healing process could take at least three years, and even after that, there was no guarantee he would be able to play sport. Nathan loved running around and was very active, so this was hard to accept.

It was a few months before Nathan could return to school. In that time, my doctors were telling me they wanted to get a sample from the lump they had found in my breast. Right away my mind went to some friends who had terrible experiences after biopsies. I refused, and said that if they wanted to touch the lump, they had to remove it totally. They said they could not do that, as Medicare would not cover it unless it was malignant and needed to be removed, so I told them they had to leave it. I was still getting the numbness in my left side, and had not been able to see the specialist about my eye while I was busy with Nathan.

In all of this I was seeking God, wondering if my time had come to an end on this earth. I didn't want to leave my children, and wondered if I should make videos or write letters for them so that if it was my time, they would always know how much I loved them. Soon after, I attended a women's conference at church where the speaker talked about people who had passed away as a result of breast cancer, or were still struggling through it. I went home and wept in Colin's arms, questioning if God was trying to prepare me for what was ahead.

As if this wasn't enough, Colin also got sick, to the point where he could barely breathe. I rushed him to the hospital where he was placed on oxygen, had x-rays taken, and found out that one of his lungs had collapsed. *Really?!* I felt anger rise in me and a fight I thought I never had, as I decided *no more*; I was not going to lay down and let this all happen. I began to fight in prayer and with the words I spoke.

Our breakthrough came when we were blessed with tickets to a conference our church was hosting. While we were there, a speaker by the name of Creflo Dollar stopped part way through his presentation, walked to the side of the stage where we were sitting, and said as he pointed in our direction, that there was a lady with a lump. He placed his hand on his body in the area where my lump was, including my glands, which were so sore and swollen. He said, "God said that the lump is healed, that by the morning it will all be gone."

I sat there, somehow knowing that word was for me, but saying, "No, there has to be someone else here that is worse than me, and it's for them." Colin kept looking at me but I would not look at him. Within minutes, however, my breast and glands were itchy, so itchy I was struggling not to scratch in public. We went home that night and sure enough, the next morning I woke up and the lump was gone. I did tell Colin then. This gave me more determination to fight for our family, and I began fasting and praying. I felt the fight in me get bigger and stronger, and I had a deep belief that all our health issues were going to be beaten. I knew it was God in me.

Soon it was time to take Nathan back for his checkup and have the cast changed to a leg boot. We kept praying for Nathan, and with him, as he struggled with not being able to do much. A few nights before his appointment, Nathan saw God heal his leg; in fact, he told us he watched God grow his bone in a dream. We all held onto that, and were delighted when the new x-rays showed that Nathan's bone was back! The doctor argued with the nurse as we sat there, determined she had x-rayed the wrong leg or got it mixed up with someone else's, but Nathan looked at the doctor with a huge smile and said, "God healed me." The doctor just smiled back at Nathan with nothing to say.

By now, Colin's lung had recovered and Nicole was better from all her allergies too. I decided that I would manage with the numbness on my left side and the spots in my eye, as we could not afford any more doctor or specialist visits. We were so thankful and grateful with what God had done, but all of this had been going on for a few months and I had reached a point where I was so tired and felt I had no more energy to take the numbness or eye condition to God in prayer again.

◆ ◆ ◆

I was still concerned with why everything had happened, however, so I continued to press into God. As I did so, He revealed that we all at times face trials, as we live in a broken world, but He also revealed that Colin was struggling with pornography again. It wasn't the same as in earlier years, but it was back regardless. When I confronted Colin that night, we had a huge argument. I cried for many nights as I wrestled with my feelings and thoughts. We spoke numerous times and I felt God tell me to pray with him and for him, which was hard, but I pushed myself to do that. I was so angry, and even though I was praying, I struggled with forgiving him. But God reminded me of Peter's question about how often we should forgive someone the same sin, and the Lord's reply that we should forgive many, many times.

Later that day when Colin came home, I was able to tell him I forgave him and when he apologised to me, I knew he meant it. That weekend at church there was a visiting speaker by the name of Allen Meyer, who introduced his book *From Good Man to Valiant Man*. A few days later, Colin felt drawn to go with a friend to a men's group that was going through the 'valiant man' course. The Holy Spirit worked deeply in and with Colin during this time. Towards the end of that year, God opened unexpected doors, and Colin was offered a new job in the state of New South Wales.

We moved to New South Wales and enrolled the kids in a government school. This went badly for our kids—the classes were blended, and the principal (who was also the teacher) did not teach or help the kids, and when I offered to help, I was told that parent help was not wanted. Nicole and Nathan lost all drive for school and were struggling to learn anything, so we moved them to another school.

Now I had to face putting the children on a bus every day. This meant I would not have much time sharing their experiences at school anymore, which I was not ready to give up, but we needed to do what was best for our kids. As I prayed for direction, I felt I needed to let go a little and trust that God would always keep them safe. One day I was placing two pictures of the children into a frame, when I looked at the images together and saw a picture of the two children in what looked like Jesus' face. I felt as if I was receiving a confirmation of what I had felt in prayer. Now I know none of us living have physically seen Jesus' face, but we often see a portrayal of His face, and this was what I saw. This strengthened my confidence, and I knew the kids would always be in Jesus, and Jesus in them. I still have the picture frame hanging on the wall as a reminder when days feel hard.

◆ ◆ ◆

We had been on the farm in New South Wales for a few months. It was harvest time, and I was offered casual work, doing various jobs. I took the work, figuring that at least I was doing something. By the third harvest season, however, my eyesight was getting worse, until one morning at work, I realised that I could not see out of that eye at all. I felt panic rising. I went to see the specialist who advised me to have an operation, but there was a risk I could haemorrhage from my eye, so I decided that was not an option I wanted to choose. The specialist put me on some drops to control the eye pressure, which was very high, and agreed to monitor me over six monthly visits. Colin and I prayed so many times for my eye, and we had others praying too, but I thought I never had enough faith. In the end I decided that if people like Lisa Bevere, who has one working eye, could manage, then I would too. I would just need to adapt a little.

But the next time I saw the specialist, I realised that many things needed to change—like driving. It appeared I would have to re-sit my test, and may not be allowed to drive, which would then put extra pressure on Colin, and on other areas of life. Once again, I decided I needed to press into God in prayer, as I never wanted this.

That week as I spent time praying, I felt the Holy Spirit stir in me a question, "Is sickness of God?" to which I replied, "No, it is not of God. I know sin, brokenness and sickness come from the fallen world and its ways, and at times from our choices." I felt the Holy Spirit then stir in me another question: "Then why are you happily accepting it?"

I began to realise that with all I had heard from the specialists, I had decided I could live with the numbness and the loss of vision in my eye. I had given up the fight and said, *Okay, you can stay*. I realised that I had even told myself that maybe this was part of God's plan—a thought process from so many years ago that had crept back in, only it was wrong thinking.

That day I realised that it was not my faith that was lacking, but my belief. What I believed did not line up with the faith I had. I chose to ask for forgiveness and healing, and decided to stop checking my eye every day to see if it was getting worse, as this was causing me to focus more and more on the negative rather than on God and the truth of His Word. I needed to get myself in alignment with Him. That day I wept with God and really felt His arms around me. Even as I slept that night, I could hear my spirit communing in prayer with God.

Because of my eye, I had stopped driving at night. A few days after that prayer time, I was in town doing shopping. The queues were so long at the checkouts that day, and it was wintertime, so it got dark early, and I had the children with me. Because I had accepted my condition until now, I had also caused my children and Colin to have fear when I drove. That night I could feel the nervousness rising in me as I could see it getting darker and I was not at the checkout yet. I thought maybe I should leave the shopping and drive home while it was still a little light. I knew that the cost of fuel to come back to town was a waste, so I stood there with my two little treasures listening to them saying, "Mom, it's getting dark. Please can we go?" I told them it would be okay.

We got to the car, and as I shop for a month at a time, there was a lot to load. When we got into the vehicle, I closed my eyes and prayed, "Lord today it ends!"

Colin called to ask if I needed him to come and drive us home, saying we could pick our vehicle up in the morning, or I could follow close behind him on the road, but I said no, it was going to be okay. My heart was beating very hard in my chest as I reversed and drove off, but I refused to be beaten by fear. Less than ten minutes into my drive, I suddenly thought, *Wow, I can see more*, and within a few more minutes, I realised I could see everything! I closed my good eye for a second and still I could see. My body had aligned with my healing! God had already done it, but my false belief and my willingness to give up had caused me to delay the healing. It was a valuable lesson and one I would never forget.

◆ ◆ ◆

We all have our own wilderness walk, and we can either allow it to grow us and correct us, or to destroy us. It's only as we begin to understand the wildernesses others have walked through and are willing to share our experiences with others, that we will be free to move forward, grow, and experience the fullness that God plans and desires for us.

Through my wilderness, I learnt that God was and is my only safe, sure, and true place. He filled—and still fills—me up. He led and continues to lead me. I learnt that I needed to have ears to hear, and a willing heart; I needed to believe and test all things with God. I often have to remind myself of these things.

My wilderness walk started as a child when I faced the consequences of others' choices. This was not what God ever wanted. But along the way, I had to learn to use my experiences to improve and better myself, my choices, and my future. As I got older, I made poor choices too, some of which have had long-term consequences. This has required dedication to working with God to get breakthrough, and to repair and remould. I have had to learn to grow into and with God, and to allow Him to grow in me so that I can live in His fullness, not my smallness. That is what each of our wilderness walks will do if we follow God wholeheartedly. Not all walks are hard and painful, and that is good too. As long as we grow with God and allow Him to use and direct us, we will see the fruits of righteous living.

STEP OUT OF THE WILDERNESS

Is there anything that you have consciously or subconsciously been trying to keep hidden? With the help of the Holy Spirit, bring it into the light and allow yourself to receive the Father's grace. Be encouraged to not let fear have a grip on you. It will most likely not be easy to face, but if you start one step at a time, you will see how the truth and God's love will set you free.

CHAPTER TEN

And this I pray, that your love may abound still more and more in knowledge and all discernment, that you may approve the things that are excellent, that you may be sincere and without offense till the day of Christ, being filled with the fruits of righteousness which are by Jesus Christ, to the glory and praise of God.
Philippians 1 v 9-11

We never stop growing and learning, and we won't stop until the day we go to be with the Lord. I have had moments however, and still do, when I feel numb in a sense, stuck in a storm with my flesh and spirit conflicting.

Lately the Holy Spirit has been revealing to me how our flesh, our situations, and the words, thoughts and actions of others and ourselves, work together to entangle us in guilt. I have found this even includes things that I know I have worked through with the Lord before, and that has confused me at times, sending me searching to see what I missed or didn't follow His leading on.

The Holy Spirit revealed that I have done what He has led me to, and the Lord has set me free, but I have not always set myself free. There are days when I remember things I have said, done or experienced before, often triggered by something I hear, see, or even smell. These flashbacks cause me to relive a situation in my mind which can give rise to guilt. In most cases, to be honest, this guilt has turned into shame, resulting in the inability to be free within myself. I learnt that the guilt came from feeling terrible about something I had done or said or been involved with. When I didn't work through the guilt, it became an area of shame, not just for what I did, but for who I now was. I had let guilt and shame define me.

I have had to work through areas with Colin where I came to realise that I still had guilt attached, and in some areas, even shame. This led to me holding back on loving myself or responding positively to Colin. I found I felt guilty if I was going to do something for myself and wondered why that feeling was rising in me.

We need to learn to align our view of ourselves with the way God sees us. We may not be perfect, but because of what Jesus achieved on the cross we are seen as righteous and clean. I felt the Holy Spirit tell me that when I don't see myself the way God sees me, then I am not acknowledging the fullness of what Jesus did and achieved on the cross for me. This has been hard, because the way I viewed myself through the guilt and shame has had a strong hold and impact on me.

Whenever I bring situations or issues to the Lord, I have to consciously remind myself how God sees me. I have even seen it in my kids, how a small decision or comment by someone else has made them feel guilty, and if they hear it again, shame can fall on them. Then, if they begin to say they are to blame, it begins to define them. Once shame begins to define a person, it has a deep attachment that is not easy to break off. I found that to break shame off me, I have had to speak God's Word over myself repeatedly, and continually remind myself that all my shame has been given to God and I have been washed clean, that I am forgiven by the Most High and therefore I need to forgive myself, that I am set free.

I have felt able to forgive myself more easily in some areas than in others. In my wilderness journey, I have found that situation by situation, God through the Holy Spirit worked with me, clearing away layer after layer until I saw myself the way I should. Learning to accept and appreciate myself has been freeing. It has helped me to break many unhealthy habits such as making jokes about myself, highlighting my own faults (which I assumed others were looking at), always apologising even if it was not something I needed to apologise for, and trying to ensure others felt good at the cost of myself.

I have learnt that the more time goes on and the more I seek God and press into Him, the easier it gets to hear the Holy Spirit's prompting. The Bible talks about the road being narrow, and as I have walked this journey, it is this narrow road that has helped to keep me on track with the Lord.

STEP OUT OF THE WILDERNESS

What has happened on your journey that you feel guilt for or that has become shameful? After starting your wilderness journey, where do you find yourself now? Be sure to acknowledge your growth; it is all a great achievement!

AUTHOR'S NOTE

In 2008 I made a friend who is a journalist, and she told me I should write a book. I laughed this idea off, thinking, *Sure, about what?* I was convinced no one else would want to hear about my experiences. Then, in 2009, a few more people said the same thing, and I thought, *Hey, maybe I should!*

I got a notebook and started to write down the things I experienced. I thought of a name for the book and wrote a page or two, read it, and realised I couldn't do it, so I let go of the idea.

Then the following year at a church conference, a speaker by the name of Myles Munroe said, "Where is that book you should have written?" It felt like he could see me in the crowd of thousands and was talking directly to me. At the end of the session, before he left the stage, he said, "Now when I come back next year, I want to see that book you are going to write."

Something in his words touched me, and I felt the stirring of God that there was a book for me to write. I had bought some of Myles Munroe's books, and went to get them signed by him and his wife. In mine, he wrote 'Philippians 1 v 6', which tells us to be confident because He who has begun a good work in us will continue to complete it until the day of Jesus Christ. He also wrote the words, 'Die Empty'. I felt God did not want me to die full of everything I was carrying—He wanted me to finish well and let Him use me as a light stand for His light to shine in a very dark place. So, I made a second attempt at writing a book, but again, my fear and doubt won out. After looking through both attempts, I decided that maybe it was not what I was supposed to do. *Did I ask God?* No!

In 2015 those stirrings rose again as God drew me back to the idea of turning my journey into a book. One night I woke up with the title of my book in my mind, and I felt a deep excitement growing. I wrote it down and went back to sleep. A few months later I woke up in the middle of the night with a picture of the cover in my mind. I began to believe that this really was what I was meant to do. In 2016, I began working on this book you now hold.

It is my prayer that, as I have shared some of the experiences and lessons of my wilderness walk, you can see the Father, Jesus, and the Holy Spirit more clearly, and that you understand more fully who He has redeemed you to be, that you are loved and adored, chosen by Him.

Yes, you will continue to face struggles, but you do not have to accept whatever does not line up with God's Word. God has a good plan and purpose for you no matter who you are. No matter what you have faced or what you have chosen before, there is hope for the days ahead because God is faithful and as you lean into Him, He will give you the victory. He's longing to lead you into the fullness of what He planned for you! I pray that the Spirit enables you to press into God and that you allow Him to be your light and guide. Don't be held back any longer by the things of your past; step into and experience the peace and freedom that can only come from God.

Brokenness is in this world, caused by wrong choices and sin, but when we look back at God's original design in the Garden of Eden, we see that nothing was broken, nothing. That was what God wanted for us because He is not broken—He is perfectly whole and complete, and because we are made in His image, we hunger for this wholeness. I personally look forward to the day that I share a space in heaven where all will be made new and there will be no more tears or suffering. It will be as God intended it from the start. In the meantime, on this earth, we can begin to realign with God's original design by keeping in step with God, asking, listening, following, and obeying His Word and leading. If we start choosing these things, they will get easier. Turning to God and relying on Him will become more instinctive.

So I urge you, keep focused on your relationship with God; continually grow in His wisdom, knowledge, understanding, and discernment of all things; and look ahead with faith as you believe and hold fast to God's Word and will for your life. Trust Him to lead you out of the wilderness, and may His work in your life become a blessing to others.

MEDITATIONS FROM GOD'S WORD

HOPE AND REASSURANCE

And the peace of God, which surpasses all understanding, will guard your hearts and minds through Christ Jesus. (Philippians 4:7)

Let your conduct be without covetousness; be content with such things as you have. For He Himself has said, "I will never leave you nor forsake you." (Hebrews 13:5)

"...teaching them to observe all things that I have commanded you; and lo, I am with you always, even to the end of the age." (Matthew 28:20)

And they prayed and said, "You, O Lord, who know the hearts of all..." (Acts 1:24)

"For My thoughts are not your thoughts, nor are your ways My ways," says the LORD. "For as the heavens are higher than the earth, so are My ways higher than your ways, and My thoughts than your thoughts..."(Isaiah 55:8-9)

Therefore we do not lose heart. Even though our outward man is perishing, yet the inward man is being renewed day by day. (2 Corinthians 4:16)

The LORD also will be a refuge for the oppressed, a refuge in times of trouble. (Psalm 9:9)

These things I have spoken to you while being present with you. But the Helper, the Holy Spirit, whom the Father will send in My name, He will teach you all things, and bring to your remembrance all things that I said to you. Peace I leave with you, My peace I give to you; not as the world gives do I give to you. Let not your heart be troubled, neither let it be afraid. (John 14:25-27)

Submit to God. Resist the devil and he will flee from you. (James 4:7)

No temptation has overtaken you except such as is common to man; but God is faithful, who will not allow you to be tempted beyond what you are able, but with the temptation will also make the way of escape, that you may be able to bear it. (1 Corinthians 10:13)

Blessed is the man who endures temptation; for when he has been approved, he will receive the crown of life which the Lord has promised to those who love Him. Let no one say when he is tempted, "I am tempted by God"; for God cannot be tempted by evil, nor does He Himself tempt anyone. But each one is tempted when he is drawn away by his own desires and enticed. Then, when desire has conceived, it gives birth to sin; and sin, when it is full-grown, brings forth death. Do not be deceived, my beloved brethren. (James 1:12-16)

We love Him because He first loved us. (1 John 4:19)

For He shall give His angels charge over you, to keep you in all your ways. In their hands they shall bear you up, lest you dash your foot against a stone. (Psalm 91:11-12)

The angel of the LORD encamps all around those who fear Him, and delivers them. (Psalm 34:7)

"My God sent His angel and shut the lions' mouths, so that they have not hurt me, because I was found innocent before Him; and also, O king, I have done no wrong before you." (Daniel 6:22)

And He said to me, "My grace is sufficient for you, for My strength is made perfect in weakness." Therefore most gladly I will rather boast in my infirmities, that the power of Christ may rest upon me. (2 Corinthians 12:9)

Then the angel who talked with me answered and said to me, "Do you not know what these are?" And I said, "No, my lord." So he answered and said to me: "This is the word of the LORD to Zerubbabel: 'Not by might nor by power, but by My Spirit,' says the LORD of hosts..." (Zechariah 4:5-6)

This I recall to my mind, therefore I have hope. Through the LORD's mercies we are not consumed, Because His compassions fail not. They are new every morning; Great is Your faithfulness. (Lamentations 3:21-23)

"Most assuredly, I say to you, he who believes in Me, the works that I do he will do also; and greater works than these he will do, because I go to My Father. And whatever you ask in My name, that I will do, that the Father may be glorified in the Son. If you ask anything in My name, I will do it..." (John 14:12-14)

For in that He Himself has suffered, being tempted, He is able to aid those who are tempted. (Hebrews 2:18)

So when this corruptible has put on incorruption, and this mortal has put on immortality, then shall be brought to pass the saying that is written: "Death is swallowed up in victory." "O Death, where is your sting? O Hades, where is your victory?" The sting of death is sin, and the strength of sin is the law. But thanks be to God, who gives us the victory through our Lord Jesus Christ. (1 Corinthians 15:54-57)

And the LORD God said, "It is not good that man should be alone; I will make him a helper comparable to him." (Genesis 2:18)

Two are better than one, because they have a good reward for their labor. For if they fall, one will lift up his companion. But woe to him who is alone when he falls, for he has no one to help him up. Again, if two lie down together, they will keep warm; But how can one be warm alone? Though one may be overpowered by another, two can withstand him. And a threefold cord is not quickly broken. *(Ecclesiastes 4:9-12)*

Houses and riches are an inheritance from fathers, but a prudent wife is from the LORD. *(Proverbs 19:14)*

Ask, and it will be given to you; seek, and you will find; knock, and it will be opened to you. For everyone who asks receives, and he who seeks finds, and to him who knocks it will be opened. *(Matthew 7:7-8)*

SALVATION AND FORGIVENESS

Jesus said to him, "I am the way, the truth, and the life. No one comes to the Father except through Me. If you had known Me, you would have known My Father also; and from now on you know Him and have seen Him." *(John 14:6-7)*

For if you forgive men their trespasses, your heavenly Father will also forgive you. But if you do not forgive men their trespasses, neither will your Father forgive your trespasses. *(Matthew 6:14-15)*

For God so loved the world that He gave His only begotten Son, that whoever believes in Him should not perish but have everlasting life. For God did not send His Son into the world to condemn the world, but that the world through Him might be saved. *(John 3:16-17)*

And He Himself is the propitiation for our sins, and not for ours only but also for the whole world. *(1 John 2:2)*

"Judge not, that you be not judged. For with what judgment you judge, you will be judged; and with the measure you use, it will be measured back to you..." *(Matthew 7:1-2)*

Then Peter came to Him and said, "Lord, how often shall my brother sin against me, and I forgive him? Up to seven times?" Jesus said to him, "I do not say to you, up to seven times, but up to seventy times seven..." (Matthew 18:21-22)

For I delivered to you first of all that which I also received: that Christ died for our sins according to the Scriptures, and that He was buried, and that He rose again the third day according to the Scriptures. (1 Corinthians 15:3-4)

And why do you look at the speck in your brother's eye, but do not consider the plank in your own eye? (Matthew 7:3)

FACING TEMPTATION

Let no one say when he is tempted, "I am tempted by God"; for God cannot be tempted by evil, nor does He Himself tempt anyone. But each one is tempted when he is drawn away by his own desires and enticed. Then, when desire has conceived, it gives birth to sin; and sin, when it is full-grown, brings forth death. (James 1:13-15)

Humble yourselves under the mighty hand of God, that He may exalt you in due time, casting all your care upon Him, for He cares for you. Be sober, be vigilant; because your adversary the devil walks about like a roaring lion, seeking whom he may devour. Resist him, steadfast in the faith, knowing that the same sufferings are experienced by your brotherhood in the world. But may the God of all grace, who called us to His eternal glory by Christ Jesus, after you have suffered a while, perfect, establish, strengthen, and settle you. (1 Peter 5:6-10)

Not that I speak in regard to need, for I have learned in whatever state I am, to be content: I know how to be abased, and I know how to abound. Everywhere and in all things I have learned both to be full and to be hungry, both to abound and to suffer need. I can do all things through Christ who strengthens me. (Philippians 4:11-13)

God is our refuge and strength, a very present help in trouble. Therefore we will not fear, even though the earth be removed, and though the mountains be carried into the midst of the sea; though its waters roar and be troubled, though the mountains shake with its swelling. Selah (Psalm 46:1-3)

Now when the tempter came to Him, he said, "If You are the Son of God, command that these stones become bread." But He answered and said, "It is written, 'Man shall not live by bread alone, but by every word that proceeds from the mouth of God.'" Then the devil took Him up into the holy city, set Him on the pinnacle of the temple, and said to Him, "If You are the Son of God, throw Yourself down. For it is written: 'He shall give His angels charge over you,' and, 'In their hands they shall bear you up, lest you dash your foot against a stone.'" Jesus said to him, "It is written again, 'You shall not tempt the LORD your God.'" Again, the devil took Him up on an exceedingly high mountain, and showed Him all the kingdoms of the world and their glory. And he said to Him, "All these things I will give You if You will fall down and worship me." Then Jesus said to him, "Away with you, Satan! For it is written, 'You shall worship the LORD your God, and Him only you shall serve.'" (Matthew 4:3-10)

When He came to the place, He said to them, "Pray that you may not enter into temptation." (Luke 22:40)

But all things that are exposed are made manifest by the light, for whatever makes manifest is light. Therefore He says: "Awake, you who sleep, arise from the dead, and Christ will give you light." (Ephesians 5:13-14)

Therefore judge nothing before the time, until the Lord comes, who will both bring to light the hidden things of darkness and reveal the counsels of the hearts. Then each one's praise will come from God. (1 Corinthians 4:5)

STRENGTH AND ENDURANCE

Yet in all these things we are more than conquerors through Him who loved us. (Romans 8:37)

Be strong and of good courage, do not fear nor be afraid of them; for the LORD your God, He is the One who goes with you. He will not leave you nor forsake you. (Deuteronomy 31:6)

And the LORD, He is the One who goes before you. He will be with you, He will not leave you nor forsake you; do not fear nor be dismayed. (Deuteronomy 31:8)

Have I not commanded you? Be strong and of good courage; do not be afraid, nor be dismayed, for the LORD your God is with you wherever you go. (Joshua 1:9)

Thus says the LORD: "Cursed is the man who trusts in man and makes flesh his strength, whose heart departs from the LORD. For he shall be like a shrub in the desert, and shall not see when good comes, but shall inhabit the parched places in the wilderness, in a salt land which is not inhabited. "Blessed is the man who trusts in the LORD, and whose hope is the LORD. For he shall be like a tree planted by the waters, which spreads out its roots by the river, and will not fear when heat comes; But its leaf will be green, and will not be anxious in the year of drought, nor will cease from yielding fruit..." (Jeremiah 17:5-8)

"Come to Me, all you who labor and are heavy laden, and I will give you rest. Take My yoke upon you and learn from Me, for I am gentle and lowly in heart, and you will find rest for your souls. For My yoke is easy and My burden is light." (Matthew 11:28-30)

Faith by itself, if it does not have works, is dead. (James 2:17)

"Let them alone. They are blind leaders of the blind. And if the blind leads the blind, both will fall into a ditch." (Matthew 15:14)

Do you not know that he who is joined to a harlot is one body with her? For "the two," He says, "shall become one flesh." (1 Corinthians 6:16)

"... 'And you shall love the LORD your God with all your heart, with all your soul, with all your mind, and with all your strength.' This is the first commandment..." (Mark 12:30)

Now it shall come to pass, if you diligently obey the voice of the LORD your God, to observe carefully all His commandments which I command you today, that the LORD your God will set you high above all nations of the earth. And all these blessings shall come upon you and overtake you, because you obey the voice of the LORD your God: Blessed shall you be in the city, and blessed shall you be in the country. Blessed shall be the fruit of your body, the produce of your ground and the increase of your herds, the increase of your cattle and the offspring of your flocks. Blessed shall be your basket and your kneading bowl. Blessed shall you be when you come in, and blessed shall you be when you go out. The LORD will cause your enemies who rise against you to be defeated before your face; they shall come out against you one way and flee before you seven ways. The LORD will command the blessing on you in your storehouses and in all to which you set your hand, and He will bless you in the land which the LORD your God is giving you. The LORD will establish you as a holy people to Himself, just as He has sworn to you, if you keep the commandments of the LORD your God and walk in His ways. (Deuteronomy 28:1-9)

In this manner, therefore, pray: Our Father in heaven, Hallowed be Your name. Your kingdom come. Your will be done on earth as it is in heaven. Give us this day our daily bread and forgive us our debts, as we forgive our debtors. And do not lead us into temptation, but deliver us from the evil one. For Yours is the kingdom and the power and the glory forever. Amen. (Matthew 6: 9-13)

Beloved, do not believe every spirit, but test the spirits, whether they are of God; because many false prophets have gone out into the world. (1 John 4:1)

But solid food belongs to those who are of full age, that is, those who by reason of use have their senses exercised to discern both good and evil. (Hebrews 5:14)

Test all things; hold fast what is good. Abstain from every form of evil. (1 Thessalonians 5:21-22)

For false christs and false prophets will rise and show great signs and wonders to deceive, if possible, even the elect. (Matthew 24:24)

After these things Jesus showed Himself again to the disciples at the Sea of Tiberias, and in this way He showed Himself: Simon Peter, Thomas called the Twin, Nathanael of Cana in Galilee, the sons of Zebedee, and two others of His disciples were together. Simon Peter said to them, "I am going fishing." They said to him, "We are going with you also." They went out and immediately got into the boat, and that night they caught nothing. (John 21:1-3)

I will give you the keys of the kingdom of heaven, and whatever you bind on earth will be bound in heaven, and whatever you loose on earth will be loosed in heaven. (Matthew 16:19)

I can do all things through Christ who strengthens me. (Philippians 4:13)

But the Helper, the Holy Spirit, whom the Father will send in My name, He will teach you all things, and bring to your remembrance all things that I said to you. (John 14:26)

And we desire that each one of you show the same diligence to the full assurance of hope until the end, that you do not become sluggish, but imitate those who through faith and patience inherit the promises. (Hebrews 6:11-12)

And let us not grow weary while doing good, for in due season we shall reap if we do not lose heart. (Galatians 6:9)

Honor your father and your mother, that your days may be long upon the land which the LORD your God is giving you. (Exodus 20:12)

Children, obey your parents in the Lord, for this is right. "Honor your father and mother," which is the first commandment with promise: "that it may be well with you and you may live long on the earth." (Ephesians 6:1-3)

But if anyone does not provide for his own, and especially for those of his household, he has denied the faith and is worse than an unbeliever. (1 Timothy 5:8)

For the husband is head of the wife, as also Christ is head of the church; and He is the Savior of the body. (Ephesians 5:23)

Admonish the young women to love their husbands, to love their children, to be discreet, chaste, homemakers, good, obedient to their own husbands, that the word of God may not be blasphemed. (Titus 2:4-5)

But Jesus knew their thoughts, and said to them: "Every kingdom divided against itself is brought to desolation, and every city or house divided against itself will not stand..." (Matthew 12:25)

For every house is built by someone, but He who built all things is God. (Hebrews 3:4)

Through wisdom a house is built, and by understanding it is established; by knowledge the rooms are filled with all precious and pleasant riches. (Proverbs 24:3-4)

As iron sharpens iron, so a man sharpens the countenance of his friend. (Proverbs 27:17)

Do not be deceived: "Evil company corrupts good habits." (1 Corinthians 15:33)

He who is of a proud heart stirs up strife, but he who trusts in the LORD will be prospered. He who trusts in his own heart is a fool, but whoever walks wisely will be delivered. He who gives to the poor will not lack, but he who hides his eyes will have many curses. (Proverbs 28:25-27)

Marriage is honorable among all, and the bed undefiled; but fornicators and adulterers God will judge. (Hebrews 13:4)

"Will a man rob God? Yet you have robbed Me! But you say, 'In what way have we robbed You?' In tithes and offerings. You are cursed with a curse, for you have robbed Me, even this whole nation. Bring all the tithes into the storehouse, that there may be food in My house, and try Me now in this," says the LORD of hosts, "if I will not open for you the windows of heaven and pour out for you such blessing that there will not be room enough to receive it. And I will rebuke the devourer for your sakes, so that he will not destroy the fruit of your ground, nor shall the vine fail to bear fruit for you in the field," says the LORD of hosts; "And all nations will call you blessed, for you will be a delightful land," says the LORD of hosts. (Malachi 3:8-12)

ACKNOWLEDGEMENTS

Firstly, and most importantly, I give thanks to God the Father, God the Son and God the Holy Spirit for their presence, guidance, patience, perseverance and love for me and for all who are in my life. I give them all the glory and honor.

Thank you to my extended family for the life we have shared. I love each and every one of you so deeply. I thank God for you all and pray He blesses each of you, every day of your lives.

Thank you to my friends for walking through the ups and downs of life. You are all treasures to me.

Special thanks to my husband and best friend, Colin, for the life we have shared and still share. Colin, you are the greatest part of my journey. We have so much still to do together, which I look forward to. Thank you for being you and for choosing to do life with me. I thank God for blessing us as a couple, and for being our rock and foundation through every season.

And finally, thank you to Nicole and Nathan for being the most wonderful children. I am blessed to have you in my life and thank God for you daily. I treasure you more than you could ever know. I am so proud of you both, and to see you love and live for God as you do keeps me in awe of you.

www.ingramcontent.com/pod-product-compliance
Lightning Source LLC
Chambersburg PA
CBHW030257010526
44107CB00053B/1748